The Bridge

The Bridge

Uniting traditions in the worshipping church

Kevin
Mayhew

Acknowledgements

The publishers wish to express their gratitude to the copyright holders who have granted permission to include their material in this book.

Every effort has been made to trace the copyright holders of all the songs in this collection and we hope that no copyright has been infringed. Apology is made and pardon sought if the contrary be the case, and a correction will be made in any reprint of this book.

Important Copyright Information

We would like to remind users of this hymnal that the reproduction of any song texts or music without the permission of the copyright holder is illegal. Details of all copyright holders are clearly indicated under each song.

Many of the song texts may be covered either by a Christian Copyright Licensing (CCL) licence or a Calamus licence. If you possess a CCL or Calamus licence, it is essential that you check your instruction manual to ensure that the song you wish to use is covered.

If you are not a member of CCL or Calamus, or the song you wish to reproduce is not covered by your licence, you must contact the copyright holder direct for their permission.

Christian Copyright Licensing (Europe) Ltd have also now introduced a Music Reproduction Licence. Again, if you hold such a licence it is essential that you check your instruction manual to ensure that the song you wish to reproduce is covered. The reproduction of any music not covered by your licence is both illegal and immoral.

If you are interested in joining CCL or Calamus they can be contacted at the following addresses:

Christian Copyright Licensing (Europe) Ltd, P.O. Box 1339, Eastbourne, East Sussex BN 21 1AD
Tel: 01323 417711, Fax: 01323 417722

Calamus, 30 North Terrace, Mildenhall, Suffolk, IP28 7AB
Tel: 01638 716579, Fax: 01638 510390

First published in Great Britain in 2001 by
KEVIN MAYHEW LIMITED
Buxhall, Stowmarket, Suffolk IP14 3BW

Compilation © Kevin Mayhew Ltd 2001

The right of Susie Hare to be identified as the compiler of this work has been asserted by her in accordance with the Copyright, Designs and Patents Act 1988.

The following editions are available:

Words edition	Catalogue No. 1400269
	ISBN No. 1 84003 668 0
	ISMN No. M 57004 804 5
Organ/choir	Catalogue No. 1400270
	ISBN No. 1 84003 669 9
	ISMN No. M 57004 805 2

Text setter: Fiona Connell Finch
Proof reader: Linda Ottewell
Cover design: Jonathan Stroulger

Printed in China

Foreword

Come, let us sing for joy to the Lord; let us shout aloud to the rock of our salvation. Let us come before him with thanksgiving and extol him with music and song.
Psalm 95:1-2.

It is inevitable that different streams of the Christian church should adopt distinctive styles of worship, thus creating their own tradition. Some churches are characterised by hymns which have stood the test of time, others by songs that were written yesterday. Neither is necessarily right or wrong but we are in danger of thinking that certain songs are exclusive to our particular tradition.

My heartfelt concern is for the many churches that seek to progress from the old but at the same time fight shy of the new. They find themselves in a gap between the two, often pursuing a style of worship that misses out on the richness of either and ends up being mediocre. We in the Christian family owe it to ourselves, and to the next generation, to embrace a greater diversity of musical expression, to be open to some 'cross-pollination' and thus to share in the blessings of God's gifts. We shall be sharing in the same songs when we worship the same Lord together in heaven; let's start now – here on earth!

The Bridge has been born out of a desire to cross the denominational, doctrinal and musical divide between churches and to provide worship leaders with a resource which aims to be imaginative, theologically sound and musically varied. It contains many hymns with which you will be familiar and alongside their original tunes, some brand-new arrangements. It also includes many songs afforded us by the powerful outpouring of contemporary songwriters.

It has been a huge privilege to put together this compilation. I pray that you will find it meaningful, challenging and refreshingly different and that it will help to bring you into the presence of him who alone is worthy of our praise.

Susie Hare

Susie Hare is Music Director of St Mary's Church,
Eastrop, Basingstoke, Hampshire.

The Bridge

1

Henry Francis Lyte

1. Abide with me,
   fast falls the eventide;
   the darkness deepens;
   Lord, with me abide:
   when other helpers fail,
   and comforts flee,
   help of the helpless,
   O abide with me.

2. Swift to its close
   ebbs out life's little day;
   earth's joys grow dim,
   its glories pass away;
   change and decay
   in all around I see;
   O thou who changest not,
   abide with me.

3. I need thy presence
   ev'ry passing hour;
   what but thy grace
   can foil the tempter's pow'r?
   Who like thyself
   my guide and stay can be?
   Through cloud and sunshine,
   Lord, abide with me.

4. I fear no foe
   with thee at hand to bless;
   ills have no weight,
   and tears no bitterness.
   Where is death's sting?
   Where, grave, thy victory?
   I triumph still,
   if thou abide with me.

5. Hold thou thy cross
   before my closing eyes;
   shine through the gloom,
   and point me to the skies;
   heav'n's morning breaks,
   and earth's vain shadows flee;
   in life, in death,
   O Lord, abide with me.

2

Graham Kendrick

1. Above the clash of creeds,
   the many voices
   that call on so many names,
   into these final days
   our God has spoken
   by sending his only Son.

   There is no other way
   by which we must be saved;
   his name is Jesus,
   the only Saviour;
   no other sinless life,
   no other sacrifice,
   in all creation
   no other way.

2. Before we called he came
   to earth from heaven,
   our maker became a man;
   when no one else could pay,
   he bought our freedom,
   exchanging his life for ours.

3. Beneath the cross of Christ
   let earth fall silent
   in awe of this mystery;
   then let this song arise
   and fill the nations:
   O hear him call, 'Come to me.'

3

Bob Baker
© 1994 Mercy/Vineyard Publishing. Administered by Copycare.

1. Abraham's Son, chosen one,
   Zion's cornerstone;
   Passover Lamb, Son of Man,
   seated upon your throne.

   Hail to the King,
   hail to the King,
   hail to the King of kings.

2. O promised seed, beneath your feet
   sin and death shall fall.
   Now through us tread the serpent's head
   till you are all in all.

Continued overleaf

3. The world's yet to see your glory,
   but you'll be revealed in pow'r,
   and you will reign with the Bride ordained
   for your consummating hour.

4 Isaac Watts
© 1997 PDI Praise/CopyCare Ltd.

1. Alas, and did my Saviour bleed
   and did my Sov'reign die?
   Would he devote that sacred head
   for such a wretch as I?
   Was it for sins that I had done
   he groaned upon the tree?
   Amazing pity, grace unknown,
   and love beyond degree.

   My God, why would you shed your blood,
   so pure and undefiled,
   to make a sinful one like me
   your chosen, precious child?

2. Well might the sun in darkness hide
   and shut his glories in,
   when Christ, the mighty Maker, died
   for man the creature's sin.
   Thus might I hide my blushing face
   while his dear cross appears;
   dissolve my heart in thankfulness
   and melt my eyes to tears.

5 William Chatterton Dix (1837-1898)

1. Alleluia, sing to Jesus!
   his the sceptre, his the throne;
   Alleluia! - his the triumph,
   his the victory alone.
   Hear the songs of holy Zion
   thunder like a mighty flood:
   'Jesus out of ev'ry nation
   has redeemed us by his blood!'

2. Alleluia! - not as orphans
   are we left in sorrow now;
   Alleluia! – he is near us;
   faith believes, nor questions how.
   Though the cloud from sight received him
   whom the angels now adore,
   shall our hearts forget his promise,
   'I am with you evermore'?

3. Alleluia! - bread of heaven,
   here on earth our food, our stay;
   Alleluia! - here the sinful
   come to you from day to day.
   Intercessor, friend of sinners,
   earth's redeemer, plead for me,
   where the songs of all the sinless
   sweep across the crystal sea.

4. Alleluia, sing to Jesus!
   his the sceptre, his the throne;
   Alleluia! his the triumph,
   his the victory alone.
   Hear the songs of holy Zion
   thunder like a mighty flood:
   'Jesus out of ev'ry nation
   has redeemed us by his blood!'

6 William John Sparrow-Simpson (1859-1952) alt.
© Novello & Co. Ltd.

1. All for Jesus! All for Jesus!
   This our song shall ever be;
   for we have no hope nor Saviour
   if we have not hope in thee.

2. All for Jesus! thou wilt give us
   strength to serve thee hour by hour;
   none can move us from thy presence
   while we trust thy love and pow'r.

3. All for Jesus! at thine altar
   thou dost give us sweet content;
   there, dear Saviour, we receive thee
   in thy holy sacrament.

4. All for Jesus! thou hast loved us,
   all for Jesus! thou hast died,
   all for Jesus! thou art with us,
   all for Jesus, glorified!

5. All for Jesus! All for Jesus!
   This the Church's song shall be,
   till at last the flock is gathered
   one in love, and one in thee.

7 Dave Moody
© 1981 Dayspring Music/Word Music/CopyCare

All hail King Jesus!
All hail Emmanuel!
King of kings, Lord of lords,
bright morning star.
And throughout eternity
I'll sing your praises,
and I'll reign with you
throughout eternity.

8 Edward Perronet

1. All hail the pow'r of Jesus' name!
   let angels prostrate fall;
   bring forth the royal diadem
   and crown him, crown him, crown him,
   crown him Lord of all.

2. Crown him, ye martyrs of your God,
   who from his altar call;
   praise him whose way of pain ye trod,
   and crown him, crown him, crown him,
   crown him Lord of all.

3. Ye prophets who our freedom won,
   ye searchers great and small,
   by whom the work of truth is done,
   now crown him, crown him, crown him,
   crown him Lord of all.

4. Ye seed of Israel's chosen race,
   ye ransomed of the fall,
   hail him who saves you by his grace,
   and crown him, crown him, crown him,
   crown him Lord of all.

5. Let ev'ry tribe and ev'ry tongue
   to him their hearts enthral;
   lift high the universal song,
   and crown him, crown him, crown him,
   crown him Lord of all.

6. O that, with yonder sacred throng,
   we at his feet may fall,
   join in the everlasting song,
   and crown him, crown him, crown him,
   crown him Lord of all.

9 Noel and Tricia Richards
© 1987 Kingsway's Thankyou Music

1. All heav'n declares
   the glory of the risen Lord.
   Who can compare
   with the beauty of the Lord?
   For ever he will be
   the Lamb upon the throne.
   I gladly bow the knee
   and worship him alone.

2. I will proclaim
   the glory of the risen Lord.
   Who once was slain
   to reconcile us to God.
   For ever you will be
   the Lamb upon the throne.
   I gladly bow the knee
   and worship you alone.

10 Graham Kendrick
© 1993 Make Way Music

1. All I once held dear,
   built my life upon,
   all this world reveres,
   and wars to own,
   all I once thought gain
   I have counted loss;
   spent and worthless now,
   compared to this.

Continued overleaf

Knowing you, Jesus, knowing you,
there is no greater thing.
You're my all, you're the best,
you're my joy, my righteousness,
and I love you, Lord.

2. Now my heart's desire
is to know you more,
to be found in you
and known as yours.
To possess by faith
what I could not earn,
all-surpassing gift
of righteousness.

3. Oh, to know the pow'r
of your risen life,
and to know you
in your sufferings.
To become like you
in your death, my Lord,
so with you to live
and never die.

11 Stuart Townend
© 1998 Kingsway's Thankyou Music

1. All my days I will sing this song of
gladness,
give my praise to the fountain of
delights;
for in my helplessness you heard my cry,
and waves of mercy poured down on my
life.

2. I will trust in the cross of my Redeemer,
I will sing of the blood that never fails,
of sins forgiven, of conscience cleansed,
of death defeated and life without end.

Beautiful Saviour, Wonderful Counsellor,
clothed in majesty, Lord of history,
you're the Way, the Truth, the Life.
Star of the Morning, glorious in holiness,
you're the risen one, heaven's champion,
and you reign, you reign over all!

3. I long to be where the praise is never-
ending,
yearn to dwell where the glory never
fades,
where countless worshippers will share
one song,
and cries of 'worthy' will honour the Lamb!

12 Robert Bridges (1844-1930), based on 'Meine Hoffnung
stehet feste' by Joachim Neander (1650-1680)
© Oxford University Press

1. All my hope on God is founded;
he doth still my trust renew.
Me through change and chance he guideth,
only good and only true.
God unknown, he alone
calls my heart to be his own.

2. Human pride and earthly glory,
sword and crown betray his trust;
what with care and toil he buildeth,
tow'r and temple, fall to dust.
But God's pow'r, hour by hour,
is my temple and my tow'r.

3. God's great goodness aye endureth,
deep his wisdom, passing thought:
splendour, light and life attend him,
beauty springeth out of naught.
Evermore, from his store,
new-born worlds rise and adore.

4. Still from earth to God eternal
sacrifice of praise be done,
high above all praises praising
for the gift of Christ his Son.
Christ doth call one and all:
ye who follow shall not fall.

13 William Kethe

1. All people that on earth do dwell,
sing to the Lord with cheerful voice;
him serve with fear, his praise forth tell,
come ye before him and rejoice.

2. Know that the Lord is God indeed,
   without our aid he did us make;
   we are his flock, he doth us feed,
   and for his sheep he doth us take.

3. O enter then his gates with praise,
   approach with joy his courts unto;
   praise, laud and bless his name always,
   for it is seemly so to do.

4. For why? the Lord our God is good:
   his mercy is for ever sure;
   his truth at all times firmly stood,
   and shall from age to age endure.

5. Praise God from whom all blessings flow,
   praise him, all creatures here below,
   praise him above, ye heav'nly hosts:
   praise Father, Son and Holy Ghost.

14
J. W. Van De Venter
© HarperCollins Religious/CopyCare

1. All to Jesus I surrender,
   all to him I freely give;
   I will ever love and trust him,
   in his presence daily live.

   I surrender all, I surrender all,
   all to thee, my blessèd Saviour,
   I surrender all.

2. All to Jesus I surrender,
   humbly at his feet I bow;
   worldly pleasures all forsaken,
   take me, Jesus, take me now.

3. All to Jesus I surrender,
   make me, Saviour, wholly thine;
   let me feel the Holy Spirit,
   truly know that thou art mine.

4. All to Jesus I surrender,
   Lord, I give myself to thee;
   fill me with thy love and power,
   let thy blessing fall on me.

5. All to Jesus I surrender,
   now to feel the sacred flame;
   O, the joy of full salvation!
   Glory, glory to his name!

15
Darlene Zschech
© 1997 Darlene Zschech/Hillsongs Publishing/Kingsway's
Thankyou Music

Almighty God, my Redeemer,
my hiding-place, my safe refuge,
no other name like Jesus,
no pow'r can stand against you.
My feet are planted on this rock
and I will not be shaken.
My hope, it comes from you alone,
my Lord, and my salvation.

Your praise is always on my lips,
your word is living in my heart
and I will praise you with a new song,
my soul will bless you, Lord.
You fill my life with greater joy,
yes, I delight myself in you
and I will praise you with a new song,
my soul will bless you, Lord.

When I am weak, you make me strong.
When I'm poor, I know I'm rich,
for in the power of your name
all things are possible,
all things are possible,
all things are possible,
all things are possible.

16
John Newton and John Rees

1. Amazing grace! How sweet the sound
   that saved a wretch like me.
   I once was lost, but now I'm found;
   was blind, but now I see.

2. 'Twas grace that taught my heart to fear,
   and grace my fears relieved.
   How precious did that grace appear
   the hour I first believed.

Continued overleaf

3. Through many dangers, toils and snares
   I have already come.
   'Tis grace that brought me safe thus far,
   and grace will lead me home.

4. The Lord has promised good to me,
   his word my hope secures;
   he will my shield and portion be
   as long as life endures.

5. Yes, when this heart and flesh shall fail,
   and mortal life shall cease,
   I shall possess within the veil
   a life of joy and peace.

6. When we've been there a thousand years,
   bright shining as the sun,
   we've no less days to sing God's praise
   than when we first begun.

17 Charles Wesley

1. And can it be that I should gain
   an int'rest in the Saviour's blood?
   Died he for me, who caused his pain?
   For me, who him to death pursued?
   Amazing love! How can it be that thou,
   my God, shouldst die for me?

2. 'Tis myst'ry all! Th'Immortal dies:
   who can explore his strange design?
   In vain the first-born seraph tries
   to sound the depths of love divine!
   'Tis mercy all! Let earth adore,
   let angel minds inquire no more.

3. He left his Father's throne above
   so free, so infinite his grace;
   emptied himself of all but love,
   and bled for Adam's helpless race;
   'tis mercy all, immense and free;
   for, O my God, it found out me.

4. Long my imprisoned spirit lay
   fast bound in sin and nature's night;
   thine eye diffused a quick'ning ray,
   I woke, the dungeon flamed with light;
   my chains fell off, my heart was free;
   I rose, went forth, and followed thee.

5. No condemnation now I dread;
   Jesus, and all in him, is mine!
   Alive in him, my living Head,
   and clothed in righteousness divine,
   bold I approach the eternal throne,
   and claim the crown, through Christ
   my own.

18 Graham Kendrick

And he shall reign for ever,
his throne and crown shall ever endure.
And he shall reign for ever,
and we shall reign with him.

1. What a vision filled my eyes,
   one like a Son of man.
   Coming with the clouds of heav'n
   he approached an awesome throne.

2. He was given sov'reign power,
   glory and authority.
   Every nation, tribe and tongue
   worshipped him on bended knee.

3. On the throne for ever,
   see the Lamb who once was slain;
   wounds of sacrificial love
   for ever shall remain.

19 William Bright (1824-1901)

1. And now, O Father, mindful of the love
   that bought us, once for all, on Calv'ry's
      tree,
   and having with us him that pleads above,
   we here present, we here spread forth to
      thee
   that only off'ring perfect in thine eyes,
   the one true, pure, immortal sacrifice.

2. Look, Father, look on his anointed face,
   and only look on us as found in him;
   look not on our misusings of thy grace,
   our prayer so languid, and our faith so dim:
   for lo, between our sins and their reward
   we set the Passion of thy Son our Lord.

3. And then for those, our dearest and our
      best,
   by this prevailing presence we appeal;
   O fold them closer to thy mercy's breast,
   O do thine utmost for their souls' true
      weal;
   from tainting mischief keep them pure
      and clear,
   and crown thy gifts with strength to
      persevere.

4. And so we come: O draw us to thy feet,
   most patient Saviour, who canst love us
      still;
   and by this food, so aweful and so sweet,
   deliver us from ev'ry touch of ill:
   in thine own service make us glad and
      free,
   and grant us never more to part with thee.

20 James Montgomery (1771-1854)

1. Angels from the realms of glory,
   wing your flight o'er all the earth;
   ye, who sang creation's story,
   now proclaim Messiah's birth:

   Come and worship,
   worship Christ, the new-born king.

2. Shepherds in the field abiding,
   watching o'er your flocks by night,
   God with man is now residing,
   yonder shines the infant light:

3. Sages, leave your contemplations;
   brighter visions beam afar;
   seek the great desire of nations;
   ye have seen his natal star:

4. Saints, before the altar bending,
   watching long with hope and fear,
   suddenly the Lord, descending,
   in his temple shall appear:

21 Francis Pott (1832-1909) alt.

1. Angel-voices ever singing
   round thy throne of light,
   angel-harps for ever ringing,
   rest not day nor night;
   thousands only live to bless thee,
   and confess thee Lord of might.

2. Thou who art beyond the farthest
   mortal eye can see,
   can it be that thou regardest
   our poor hymnody?
   Yes, we know that thou art near us
   and wilt hear us constantly.

3. Yea, we know that thou rejoicest
   o'er each work of thine;
   thou didst ears and hands and voices
   for thy praise design;
   craftsman's art and music's measure
   for thy pleasure all combine.

4. In thy house, great God, we offer
   of thine own to thee;
   and for thine acceptance proffer,
   all unworthily,
   hearts and minds and hands and voices
   in our choicest psalmody.

5. Honour, glory, might and merit
   thine shall ever be,
   Father, Son and Holy Spirit,
   blessèd Trinity.
   Of the best that thou hast given
   earth and heaven render thee.

22 Martin J. Nystrom

1. As the deer pants for the water,
   so my soul longs after you.
   You alone are my heart's desire
   and I long to worship you.

   You alone are my strength, my shield,
   to you alone may my spirit yield.
   You alone are my heart's desire
   and I long to worship you.

2. I want you more than gold or silver,
   only you can satisfy.
   You alone are the real joy-giver
   and the apple of my eye.

3. You're my friend and you are my brother,
   even though you are a King.
   I love you more than any other,
   so much more than anything.

23 Lex Loizides

1. As we see the world in tatters,
   as we watch their dreams break down,
   we can hear their quiet anguish:
   'Come and help us!'
   Brought to life by God's own Spirit,
   joined together in his Son,
   now the church with strength arises
   like an army.

   Ev'ry place, ev'ry place
   where our feet shall tread,
   ev'ry tribe, ev'ry race
   God has given us

2. In the midst of boastful darkness
   shines a light that cannot fail,
   and the blind behold his glory,
   Jesus! Jesus!
   Not content with restoration
   of the remnant in the land,
   he has filled us with his power
   for the nations.

24 Stuart Dauermann

1. At all times I will bless him,
   his praise will be in my mouth -
   my soul makes its boast in the Lord.
   The humble man will hear of him,
   the afflicted will be glad
   and join with me to magnify the Lord.

   Let us exalt his name together for ever -
   I sought the Lord, he heard me and
        delivered me from my fears;
   let us exalt his name together for ever -
   O sing his praises, magnify the Lord.

2. The angel of the Lord encamps
   round those who fear his name,
   to save them and deliver them from
        harm.
   Though lions roar with hunger,
   we lack for no good thing:
   no wonder, then, we praise him with our
        song.

3. Come, children, now and hear me
   if you would see long life:
   just keep your lips from wickedness and
        lies.
   Do good and turn from evil,
   seek peace instead of strife,
   love righteousness
   and God will hear your cry.

25 Caroline Maria Noel (1817-1877)

1. At the name of Jesus
   ev'ry knee shall bow,
   ev'ry tongue confess him
   King of glory now;
   'tis the Father's pleasure
   we should call him Lord,
   who, from the beginning,
   was the mighty Word.

2. At his voice creation
   sprang at once to sight,
   all the angels' faces,
   all the hosts of light,
   thrones and dominations,
   stars upon their way,
   all the heav'nly orders
   in their great array.

3. Humbled for a season,
   to receive a name
   from the lips of sinners
   unto whom he came,
   faithfully he bore it,
   spotless to the last,
   brought it back victorious
   when from death he passed.

4. Bore it up triumphant,
   with its human light,
   through all ranks of creatures
   to the central height,
   to the throne of Godhead,
   to the Father's breast,
   filled it with the glory
   of that perfect rest.

5. All creation, name him,
   with love as strong as death;
   but with awe and wonder,
   and with bated breath.
   He is God the Saviour,
   he is Christ the Lord,
   ever to be worshipped,
   trusted and adored.

6. In your hearts enthrone him;
   there let him subdue
   all that is not holy,
   all that is not true;
   crown him as your captain
   in temptation's hour;
   let his will enfold you
   in its light and pow'r.

7. Truly, this Lord Jesus
   shall return again,
   with his Father's glory,
   with his angel train;
   for all wreaths of empire
   meet upon his brow,
   and our hearts confess him
   King of glory now.

26 Graham Kendrick
© 1988 Make Way Music

At this time of giving,
gladly now we bring
gifts of goodness and mercy
from a heav'nly King.

1. Earth could not contain the treasures
   heaven holds for you,
   perfect joy and lasting pleasures,
   love so strong and true.

2. May his tender love surround you
   at this Christmastime;
   may you see his smiling face
   that in the darkness shines.

3. But the many gifts he gives
   are all poured out from one;
   come, receive the greatest gift,
   the gift of God's own Son.

   Lai, lai, lai . . .

27 David Fellingham
© 1982 Kingsway's Thankyou Music

1. At your feet we fall,
   mighty risen Lord,
   as we come before your throne
   to worship you.
   By your Spirit's pow'r
   you now draw our hearts,
   and we hear your voice
   in triumph ringing clear.

Continued overleaf

I am he that liveth,
that liveth and was dead.
Behold, I am alive for evermore.

2. There we see you stand,
   mighty risen Lord,
   clothed in garments pure and holy,
   shining bright.
   Eyes of flashing fire,
   feet like burnished bronze,
   and the sound of many waters
   is your voice.

3. Like the shining sun
   in its noonday strength,
   we now see the glory
   of your wondrous face.
   Once that face was marred,
   but now you're glorified,
   and your words like a two-edged sword
   have mighty pow'r.

28 Nathan Fellingham
© 1999 Kingsway's Thankyou Music

1. Awake, awake, O Zion,
   and clothe yourself with strength,
   shake off your dust and fix your eyes on
      him.
   For you have been redeemed by
   the precious blood of Jesus,
   and now you sit enthroned with him.

   Our God reigns, he is king of all the earth,
   our God reigns, and he's seated on the throne.
   Lift your voice and sing a song of praise,
   our God reigns, the awesome Lord most high.

2. How beautiful the feet are
   of those who bring good news,
   for they proclaim the peace that comes
      from God.
   Rise up you holy nation,
   proclaim the great salvation,
   and say to Zion: 'Your God reigns'.
   Emmanuel, Emmanuel,
   our God is with us now.

3. The watchmen lift their voices,
   and raise a shout of joy,
   for he will come again.
   Then all eyes will see the
   salvation of our God,
   for he has redeemed Jerusalem.

29 Darlene Zschech
© 1997 Darlene Zschech/Hillsongs Publishing/Kingsway's Thankyou Music

Beautiful Lord, wonderful Saviour,
I know for sure all of my days are
held in your hand, crafted into
your perfect plan.

You gently call me into your presence,
guiding me by your Holy Spirit;
teach me, dear Lord, to live all of my life
through your eyes.

I'm captured by your holy calling,
set me apart, I know you're drawing me
   to yourself;
lead me, Lord, I pray.

Take me, mould me,
use me, fill me;
I give my life to the Potter's hand.
Call me, guide me,
lead me, walk beside me;
I give my life to the Potter's hand.

30 Charitie L Bancroft
© 1997 PDI Worship. Administered by CopyCare

1. Before the throne of God above
   I have a strong, a perfect plea,
   a great High Priest whose name is Love,
   who ever lives and pleads for me.
   My name is graven on his hands,
   my name is written on his heart;
   I know that while in heav'n he stands
   no tongue can bid me thence depart,
   no tongue can bid me thence depart.

2. When Satan tempts me to despair,
   and tells me of the guilt within,
   upward I look and see him there
   who made an end to all my sin.
   Because the sinless Saviour died,
   my sinful soul is counted free;
   for God the Just is satisfied
   to look on him and pardon me,
   to look on him and pardon me.

3. Behold him there! The risen Lamb,
   my perfect, spotless righteousness;
   the great unchangeable I Am,
   the King of glory and of grace!
   One with himself I cannot die,
   my soul is purchased with his blood;
   my life is hid with Christ on high,
   with Christ my Saviour and my God.

31 Russell Fragar
© 1996 Russell Fragar/Hillsongs Publishing/Kingsway's
Thankyou Music

Before the world began
you were on his mind,
and ev'ry tear you cry
is precious in his eyes.
Because of his great love,
he gave his only Son;
ev'rything was done,
so you would come.

Nothing you can do
could make him love you more,
and nothing that you've done
could make him close the door.
Because of his great love,
he gave his only Son;
ev'rything was done
so you would come.

Come to the Father
though your gift is small,
broken hearts, broken lives,
he will take them all.
The power of the word,
the power of his blood,
everything was done
so you would come.

32 Elizabeth Cecilia Clephane (1830-1869)

1. Beneath the cross of Jesus
   I fain would take my stand;
   the shadow of a mighty rock
   within a weary land.
   A home within a wilderness,
   a rest upon the way,
   from the burning of the noontide heat
   and the burden of the day.

2. Upon that cross of Jesus
   mine eye, at times, can see
   the very dying form of one
   who suffered there for me.
   And from my stricken heart, with tears
   two wonders I confess:
   the wonders of redeeming love,
   and my own unworthiness.

3. I take, O cross, thy shadow,
   for my abiding place!
   I ask no other sunshine than
   the sunshine of his face;
   content to let the world go by,
   to know no gain nor loss:
   my sinful self my only shame,
   my glory all, the cross.

33 David J. Evans
© 1986 Kingsway's Thankyou Music

1. Be still, for the presence of the Lord,
   the Holy One is here.
   Come, bow before him now,
   with reverence and fear.
   In him no sin is found,
   we stand on holy ground.
   Be still, for the presence of the Lord,
   the Holy One is here.

Continued overleaf

2. Be still, for the glory of the Lord
   is shining all around;
   he burns with holy fire,
   with splendour he is crowned.
   How awesome is the sight,
   our radiant King of light!
   Be still, for the glory of the Lord
   is shining all around.

3. Be still, for the power of the Lord
   is moving in this place;
   he comes to cleanse and heal,
   to minister his grace.
   No work too hard for him,
   in faith receive from him.
   Be still, for the power of the Lord
   is moving in this place.

34 Katharina Von Schlegal trans. Jane L. Borthwick, alt.

1. Be still, my soul:
   the Lord is on your side;
   bear patiently the cross
   of grief and pain;
   leave to your God
   to order and provide;
   in ev'ry change
   he faithful will remain.
   Be still, my soul:
   your best, your heav'nly friend,
   through thorny ways,
   leads to a joyful end.

2. Be still, my soul:
   your God will undertake
   to guide the future
   as he has the past.
   Your hope, your confidence
   let nothing shake,
   all now mysterious
   shall be clear at last.
   Be still, my soul:
   the tempests still obey
   his voice, who ruled them
   once on Galilee.

3. Be still, my soul:
   the hour is hastening on
   when we shall be
   for ever with the Lord,
   when disappointment,
   grief and fear are gone,
   sorrow forgotten,
   love's pure joy restored.
   Be still, my soul:
   when change and tears are past,
   all safe and blessèd
   we shall meet at last.

35 Kim Noblitt
© 1997 Integrity's Praise! Music/Kingsway's Thankyou Music

1. Be still my soul, be still my soul;
   cease from the labour and the toil.
   Refreshing springs of peace await;
   to troubled minds and hearts that ache.

   Be still my soul, God knows your way;
   and he will guide for his name's sake.
   Plunge in the rivers of his grace;
   rest in the arms of his embrace.

2. Be still my soul, be still my soul;
   though battles round you rage and roar.
   One thing you need and nothing more;
   to hear the whisper of your Lord.

   Be still, my child, I know your way;
   and I will guide for my name's sake.
   Plunge in the rivers of my grace;
   rest in the arms of my embrace.

36 Irish trans. Mary Byrne and Eleanor Hull
© Copyright control

Use these words when the tune Slane (Tune 1)
is used

1. Be thou my vision,
   O Lord of my heart,
   naught be all else to me,
   save that thou art;
   thou my best thought
   in the day and the night,
   waking or sleeping,
   thy presence my light.

2. Be thou my wisdom,
   be thou my true word,
   I ever with thee
   and thou with me, Lord;
   thou my great Father,
   and I thy true heir;
   thou in me dwelling,
   and I in thy care.

3. Be thou my breastplate,
   my sword for the fight,
   be thou my armour,
   and be thou my might,
   thou my soul's shelter,
   and thou my high tow'r,
   raise thou me heav'nward,
   O Pow'r of my pow'r.

4. Riches I need not,
   nor all the world's praise,
   thou my inheritance
   through all my days;
   thou, and thou only,
   the first in my heart,
   high King of heaven,
   my treasure thou art!

5. High King of heaven,
   when battle is done,
   grant heaven's joys to me,
   O bright heav'n's sun;
   Christ of my own heart,
   whatever befall,
   still be my vision,
   O Ruler of all.

Use these words when tune 2 is used

1. Be thou my vision,
   O Lord of my heart,
   be all else but naught to me,
   save that thou art;
   be thou my best thought
   in the day and the night,
   both waking and sleeping,
   thy presence my light.

2. Be thou my wisdom,
   be thou my true word,
   be thou ever with me
   and I with thee, Lord;
   be thou my great Father,
   and I thy true heir;
   be thou in me dwelling,
   and I in thy care.

3. Be thou my breastplate,
   my sword for the fight;
   be thou my whole armour,
   be thou my true might;
   be thou my soul's shelter,
   be thou my strong tower;
   O raise thou me heavenward,
   great Power of my power.

4. Riches I need not,
   nor all the world's praise;
   be thou mine inheritance
   now and always;
   be thou and thou only,
   the first in my heart;
   O Sovereign of heaven,
   my treasure thou art.

5. High King of heaven,
   thou heaven's bright sun,
   O grant me its joys
   after vict'ry is won;
   great heart of my own heart,
   whatever befall,
   still thou be my vision,
   O Ruler of all.

37 Frances Jane van Alstyne

1. Blessèd assurance, Jesus is mine:
   O what a foretaste of glory divine!
   Heir of salvation, purchase of God;
   born of his Spirit, washed in his blood.

   This is my story, this is my song,
   praising my Saviour all the day long.

Continued overleaf

2. Perfect submission, perfect delight,
visions of rapture burst on my sight;
angels descending, bring from above
echoes of mercy, whispers of love.

This is my story, this is my song,
praising my Saviour all the day long.

3. Perfect submission, all is at rest,
I in my Saviour am happy and blessed;
watching and waiting, looking above,
filled with his goodness, lost in his love.

38 Gary Sadler and Jamie Harvill
© 1992 Integrity's Praise! Music/Kingsway's Thankyou Music

Blessing and honour, glory and power
be unto the Ancient of Days;
from ev'ry nation, all of creation
bow before the Ancient of Days.

Ev'ry tongue in heaven and earth
shall declare your glory,
ev'ry knee shall bow at your throne
in worship;
you will be exalted, O God,
and your kingdom shall not pass away,
O Ancient of Days.

Your kingdom shall reign over all the
earth:
sing unto the Ancient of Days.
For none shall compare to your matchless
worth:
sing unto the Ancient of Days.

39 Mary A Lathbury (1841-1913)

1. Break thou the Bread of Life,
dear Lord, to me,
as thou didst break the loaves
beside the sea:
beyond the sacred page
I seek thee, Lord;
my spirit pants for thee,
O living Word.

2. Thou art the Bread of Life,
O Lord, to me,
thy holy word the truth
that saveth me;
give me to eat and live
with thee above,
teach me to love thy truth,
for thou art love.

3. O send thy Spirit, Lord,
now unto me,
that he may touch my eyes
and make me see;
show me the truth concealed
within thy word,
and in thy book revealed,
I see thee, Lord.

4. Bless thou the truth, dear Lord,
to me, to me,
as thou didst bless the loaves
by Galilee;
then shall all bondage cease,
all fetters fall,
and I shall find my peace,
my all in all.

40 Edwin Hatch (1835-1889) Adapted by David Fellingham
© 1995 Kingsway's Thankyou Music

1. Breathe on me, Breath of God,
and fill my life anew;
that I may love as you love,
and do the works that you do.
Holy Spirit, breathe on me.

And let ev'ry part of me
glow with fire divine;
with passion in my life,
Jesus let your glory shine.

2. Breathe on me, Breath of God,
until my heart is pure;
until my will is one with yours
let holiness and love endure.
Holy Spirit, breathe on me.

41 Edwin Hatch

1. Breathe on me, Breath of God,
   fill me with life anew,
   that I may love what thou dost love,
   and do what thou wouldst do.

2. Breathe on me, Breath of God,
   until my heart is pure:
   until with thee I have one will
   to do and to endure.

3. Breathe on me, Breath of God,
   till I am wholly thine,
   until this earthly part of me
   glows with thy fire divine.

4. Breathe on me, Breath of God,
   so shall I never die,
   but live with thee the perfect life
   of thine eternity.

42 Susie Hare
© 2001 Kevin Mayhew Ltd.

1. Broken and melted by your potter's
     hand,
   the barriers no longer hide me.
   Moulded and recreated, now I stand;
   your Spirit's love has set me free.

   And as I come before your throne,
   I worship you and you alone,
   for all the love that you have shown;
   a love that takes me just the way I am.
   The past is done and all that bound me
   is now surrendered at your feet.
   The past is done I am forgiven
   and now in you I stand complete.

2. Broken for ever are the chains that held
   the life which once was cold before you.
   Yielding to you, a heart which once
     rebelled;
   your Spirit's love has made me new.

43 Janet Lunt
© 1978 Sovereign Music UK

Broken for me, broken for you,
the body of Jesus, broken for you.

1. He offered his body, he poured out his soul;
   Jesus was broken, that we might be whole.

2. Come to my table and with me dine;
   eat of my bread and drink of my wine.

3. This is my body given for you;
   eat it remembering I died for you.

4. This is my blood I shed for you,
   for your forgiveness, making you new.

44 Noel and Tricia Richards
© 1989 Kingsway's Thankyou Music

By your side I would stay;
in your arms I would lay.
Jesus, lover of my soul,
nothing from you I withhold.

Lord, I love you, and adore you;
what more can I say?
You cause my love to grow stronger
with ev'ry passing day.

(Repeat)

45 Susie Hare
© 2001 Kevin Mayhew Ltd.

1. Chosen to go, chosen to do,
   chosen to speak your salvation;
   we are your hands,
   we are your feet,
   we are your voice in this nation.
   You're the rock on which we stand,
   make us faithful in this land
   to build up the church that you have
     planned.

   Send us out to proclaim your kingdom,
   send us out to proclaim your word.
   Send us out to proclaim your freedom,
   send us in power, O God.

Continued overleaf

2. Chosen to go, chosen to do,
   chosen to be on your mission;
   we want to give,
   we want to serve,
   we want to follow your vision.
   Where lives hide in shades of night,
   we will march in armour bright,
   taking to the dark your shining light!

   Send us out to proclaim your kingdom,
   send us out to proclaim your word.
   Send us out to proclaim your freedom,
   send us in power, O God.

3. Chosen to go, chosen to do,
   chosen to stir a desire;
   we want to reach,
   we want to build,
   we want to see hearts on fire.
   Voices raised to fill the sky,
   vict'ry's banner we shall fly,
   lifting up the name of Jesus high!

46 John Byrom (1692-1763) alt.

1. Christians, awake! salute the happy
      morn,
   whereon the Saviour of the world was
      born;
   rise to adore the mystery of love,
   which hosts of angels chanted from
      above:
   with them the joyful tidings first begun
   of God incarnate and the Virgin's Son.

2. Then to the watchful shepherds it was
      told,
   who heard th' angelic herald's voice,
      'Behold,
   I bring good tidings of a Saviour's birth
   to you and all the nations on the earth:
   this day hath God fulfilled his promised
      word,
   this day is born a Saviour, Christ the
      Lord.'

3. He spake; and straightway the celestial
      choir
   in hymns of joy, unknown before,
      conspire;
   the praises of redeeming love they sang,
   and heav'n's whole orb with alleluias rang:
   God's highest glory was their anthem still,
   peace on the earth, in ev'ry heart good will.

4. To Bethl'em straight th'enlightened
      shepherds ran,
   to see, unfolding, God's eternal plan,
   and found, with Joseph and the blessèd
      maid,
   her Son, the Saviour, in a manger laid:
   then to their flocks, still praising God,
      return,
   and their glad hearts with holy rapture
      burn.

5. O may we keep and ponder in our mind
   God's wondrous love in saving lost mankind;
   trace we the babe, who hath retrieved our
      loss,
   from his poor manger to his bitter cross;
   tread in his steps assisted by his grace,
   till our first heav'nly state again takes place.

6. Then may we hope, th'angelic hosts
      among,
   to sing, redeemed, a glad triumphal song:
   he that was born upon this joyful day
   around us all his glory shall display;
   saved by his love, incessant we shall sing
   eternal praise to heav'n's almighty King.

47 'Urbs beata Jerusalem', (c.7th century) trans. John Mason Neale (1818-1866) alt.

1. Christ is made the sure foundation,
   Christ the head and cornerstone,
   chosen of the Lord, and precious,
   binding all the Church in one,
   holy Zion's help for ever,
   and her confidence alone.

2. To this temple, where we call you,
   come, O Lord of hosts, today;
   you have promised loving kindness,
   hear your servants as we pray,
   bless your people now before you,
   turn our darkness into day.

3. Hear the cry of all your people,
   what they ask and hope to gain;
   what they gain from you, for ever
   with your chosen to retain,
   and hereafter in your glory
   evermore with you to reign.

4. Praise and honour to the Father,
   praise and honour to the Son,
   praise and honour to the Spirit,
   ever Three and ever One,
   One in might and One in glory,
   while unending ages run.

48 Michael Saward (b. 1932)
© *Michael Saward/Jubilee Hymns*

1. Christ triumphant, ever reigning,
   Saviour, Master, King.
   Lord of heav'n, our lives sustaining,
   hear us as we sing:

   Yours the glory and the crown,
   the high renown, th'eternal name.

2. Word incarnate, truth revealing,
   Son of Man on earth!
   Pow'r and majesty concealing
   by your humble birth:

3. Suff'ring servant, scorned, ill-treated,
   victim crucified!
   Death is through the cross defeated,
   sinners justified:

4. Priestly King, enthroned for ever
   high in heav'n above!
   Sin and death and hell shall never
   stifle hymns of love:

5. So, our hearts and voices raising
   through the ages long,
   ceaselessly upon you gazing,
   this shall be our song:

49 Graham Kendrick
© *1989 Make Way Music*

1. Come and see, come and see,
   come and see the King of love;
   see the purple robe
   and crown of thorns he wears.
   Soldiers mock, rulers sneer
   as he lifts the cruel cross;
   lone and friendless now,
   he climbs towards the hill.

   We worship at your feet,
   where wrath and mercy meet,
   and a guilty world
   is washed by love's pure stream.
   For us he was made sin —
   oh, help me take it in.
   Deep wounds of love
   cry out 'Father, forgive.'
   I worship, I worship
   the Lamb who was slain.

2. Come and weep, come and mourn
   for your sin that pierced him there;
   so much deeper
   than the wounds of thorn and nail.
   All our pride, all our greed,
   all our fallenness and shame;
   and the Lord has laid
   the punishment on him.

3. Man of heaven, born to earth
   to restore us to your heaven.
   Here we bow in awe
   beneath your searching eyes.
   From your tears comes our joy,
   from your death our life shall spring;
   by your resurrection power
   we shall rise.

50
Bianco da Siena trans. Richard F. Littledale

1. Come down, O Love divine,
seek thou this soul of mine,
and visit it with
thine own ardour glowing;
O Comforter, draw near,
within my heart appear,
and kindle it,
thy holy flame bestowing.

2. O let it freely burn,
till earthly passions turn
to dust and ashes
in its heat consuming;
and let thy glorious light
shine ever on my sight,
and clothe me round,
the while my path illuming.

3. Let holy charity
mine outward vesture be,
and lowliness become
mine inner clothing;
true lowliness of heart,
which takes the humbler part,
and o'er its own shortcomings
weeps with loathing.

4. And so the yearning strong,
with which the soul will long,
shall far outpass
the pow'r of human telling;
nor can we guess its grace,
till we become the place
wherein the Holy Spirit
makes his dwelling.

51
Isaac Watts (1674-1748) alt.

1. Come, let us join our cheerful songs
with angels round the throne;
ten thousand thousand are their tongues,
but all their joys are one.

2. 'Worthy the Lamb that died,' they cry,
'to be exalted thus.'
'Worthy the Lamb,' our lips reply,
'for he was slain for us.'

3. Jesus is worthy to receive
honour and pow'r divine;
and blessings, more than we can give,
be, Lord, for ever thine.

4. Let all creation join in one
to bless the sacred name
of him that sits upon the throne,
and to adore the Lamb.

52
Robert Walmsley (1831-1905)

1. Come, let us sing of a wonderful love,
tender and true;
out of the heart of the Father above,
streaming to me and to you:
wonderful love
dwells in the heart of the Father above.

2. Jesus, the Saviour, this gospel to tell,
joyfully came;
came with the helpless and hopeless to
dwell,
sharing their sorrow and shame;
seeking the lost,
saving, redeeming at measureless cost.

3. Jesus is seeking the wanderers yet;
why do they roam?
Love only waits to forgive and forget;
home! weary wanderers, home!
Wonderful love
dwells in the heart of the Father above.

4. Come to my heart, O thou wonderful
love,
come and abide,
lifting my life till it rises above
envy and falsehood and pride;
seeking to be
lowly and humble, a learner of thee.

53

Brian Doerkson
© 1998 Vineyard Songs (UK/Eire)

Come, now is the time to worship.
Come, now is the time to give your heart.
Come, just as you are to worship.
Come, just as you are before your God,
    come.

One day every tongue will confess you
    are God,
one day every knee will bow.
Still, the greatest treasure remains for
    those
who gladly choose you now.

54

Patricia Morgan and Dave Bankhead
© 1984 Kingsway's Thankyou Music

Come on and celebrate
his gift of love, we will celebrate
the Son of God who loved us
and gave us life.
We'll shout your praise, O King,
you give us joy nothing else can bring,
we'll give to you our offering
in celebration praise.

Come on and celebrate, celebrate,
celebrate and sing,
celebrate and sing to the King.
Come on and celebrate, celebrate,
celebrate and sing,
celebrate and sing to the King.

55

Susie Hare
© 2001 Kevin Mayhew Ltd.

Come, rest in the love of Jesus,
come, rest and refresh your soul;
be still as his peace enfolds you,
he will make you whole.
Give him the things that you need not
    carry,
he will bear them for you;
all of your fears to him surrender,
see what his love can do.

Come, rest in the love of Jesus,
come, rest and refresh your soul;
be still as his peace enfolds you,
he will make you whole.

56

Henry Alford (1810-1871) alt.

1. Come, ye thankful people, come,
   raise the song of harvest-home!
   All is safely gathered in,
   ere the winter storms begin;
   God, our maker, doth provide
   for our wants to be supplied;
   come to God's own temple, come;
   raise the song of harvest-home!

2. We ourselves are God's own field,
   fruit unto his praise to yield;
   wheat and tares together sown,
   unto joy or sorrow grown;
   first the blade and then the ear,
   then the full corn shall appear:
   grant, O harvest Lord, that we
   wholesome grain and pure may be.

3. For the Lord our God shall come,
   and shall take his harvest home,
   from his field shall purge away
   all that doth offend, that day;
   give his angels charge at last
   in the fire the tares to cast,
   but the fruitful ears to store
   in his garner evermore.

4. Then, thou Church triumphant, come,
   raise the song of harvest-home;
   all be safely gathered in,
   free from sorrow, free from sin,
   there for ever purified
   in God's garner to abide:
   come, ten thousand angels, come,
   raise the glorious harvest-home!

57
Chris Bowater and Ian Taylor
© 1998 Sovereign Lifestyle Music Ltd.

1. Creation is awaiting the return of the
    King.
   The trees are poised to clap their hands
     for joy.
   The mountains stand majestic to salute
     their God;
   the desert lies in wait to burst into
     bloom.

   The King is coming,
   the King is coming,
   the King is coming to set creation free.
   (Repeat)

2. The church is awaiting the return of the
    King.
   The people joined together in his love.
   Redeemed by his blood,
   washed in his word.
   As a bride longs for her bridegroom
   the church looks to God.

   The King is coming,
   the King is coming,
   the King is coming to receive his bride.
   (Repeat)

3. The world is awaiting the return of the
    King.
   The earth is a footstool for his feet.
   Ev'ry knee will bow down,
   ev'ry tongue confess,
   that Jesus Christ is Lord
   of heaven and earth.

   The King is coming,
   the King is coming,
   the King is coming to reign in majesty.
   (Repeat)

58
Martin Leckebusch
© 2001 Kevin Mayhew Ltd.

1. Creation sings! each plant and tree,
   each bird and beast in harmony;
   the brightest star, the smallest cell,
   God's tender care and glory tell.
   From ocean depths to mountain peaks,
   in praise of God, creation speaks!

2. Creation speaks a message true,
   reminds us we are creatures, too:
   to serve as stewards is our role,
   despite our dreams of full control -
   when we disparage what God owns,
   in turmoil, all creation groans.

3. Creation groans to see the day
   which ends all bondage, all decay:
   frustrated now, it must await
   the Lord who comes to recreate
   till round the universe there rings
   the song his new creation sings!

59
Matthew Bridges

1. Crown him with many crowns,
   the Lamb upon his throne;
   hark, how the heav'nly anthem drowns
   all music but its own:
   awake, my soul, and sing
   of him who died for thee,
   and hail him as thy matchless King
   through all eternity.

2. Crown him the Lord of life,
   who triumphed o'er the grave,
   and rose victorious in the strife
   for those he came to save.
   His glories now we sing,
   who died and rose on high;
   who died eternal life to bring,
   and lives that death may die.

3. Crown him the Lord of love;
   behold his hands and side,
   rich wounds, yet visible above,
   in beauty glorified:
   no angel in the sky
   can fully bear that sight,
   but downward bends each burning eye
   at mysteries so bright.

4. Crown him the Lord of peace,
   whose pow'r a sceptre sways
   from pole to pole, that wars may cease,
   and all be prayer and praise:
   his reign shall know no end,
   and round his piercèd feet
   fair flow'rs of paradise extend
   their fragrance ever sweet.

5. Crown him the Lord of years,
   the Potentate of time,
   Creator of the rolling spheres,
   ineffably sublime.
   All hail, Redeemer, hail!
   for thou hast died for me;
   thy praise shall never, never fail
   throughout eternity.

60 John Greenleaf Whittier

1. Dear Lord and Father of mankind,
   forgive our foolish ways!
   Reclothe us in our rightful mind,
   in purer lives thy service find,
   in deeper rev'rence praise,
   in deeper rev'rence praise.

2. In simple trust like theirs who heard,
   beside the Syrian sea,
   the gracious calling of the Lord,
   let us, like them, without a word,
   rise up and follow thee,
   rise up and follow thee.

3. O Sabbath rest by Galilee!
   O calm of hills above,
   where Jesus knelt to share with thee
   the silence of eternity,
   interpreted by love,
   interpreted by love!

4. Drop thy still dews of quietness,
   till all our strivings cease;
   take from our souls the strain and stress,
   and let our ordered lives confess
   the beauty of thy peace,
   the beauty of thy peace.

5. Breathe through the heats of our desire
   thy coolness and thy balm;
   let sense be dumb, let flesh retire;
   speak through the earthquake, wind
     and fire,
   O still small voice of calm,
   O still small voice of calm!

61 Charles Wesley (1707-1788) adapted by Bob Kauflin
© This version 1997 PDI Praise

1. Depth of mercy! Can there be
   mercy reaching even me?
   God, the just, his wrath forebears,
   me, the chief of sinners spares.
   So many times my heart has strayed
   from his kind and perfect ways,
   making clear my desp'rate need
   for his blood poured out for me.

2. Give me grace, Lord, let me own
   all the wrongs that I have done.
   Let me now my sins deplore,
   look to you and sin no more.
   There, for me, the Saviour stands
   holding forth his wounded hands,
   scars which ever cry for me;
   once condemned but now set free.

62
Susie Hare
© 2001 Kevin Mayhew Ltd.

1. Don't let me waste your sacrifice,
   don't let me waste your sinless life;
   all that I am must always be
   worthy of all you gave for me.
   When I forget the Father's loss,
   lift up my eyes to see your cross;
   show me the pain of Calvary,
   Jesus you did it all for me.

   I want to rebuild the altar of my heart,
   give you my first and give you my last,
   yours is the death that brought me life;
   don't let me waste your sacrifice,
   don't let me waste your sacrifice.

2. When I forget to see your throne,
   show me the thorns that made your
       crown;
   when I forget the tears you cried,
   show me the wounds that marred your side.
   You didn't die that I might still
   hold to a life that binds your will;
   don't let me waste the price you paid,
   I want to walk the path you made.

63
Andy Park
© 1994 Mercy/Vineyard Publishing/CopyCare

1. Down the mountain the river flows,
   and it brings refreshing wherever it goes.
   Through the valleys and over the fields,
   the river is rushing and the river is here.

   The river of God sets our feet a-dancing,
   the river of God fills our hearts with cheer;
   the river of God fills our mouths with
   laughter,
   and we rejoice for the river is here.

2. The river of God is teeming with life,
   and all who touch it can be revived.
   And those who linger on this river's shore
   will come back thirsting for more of the
       Lord.

3. Up to the mountain we love to go
   to find the presence of the Lord.
   Along the banks of the river we run,
   we dance with laughter, giving praise to
       the Son.

64
Geoff and Judith Roberts
© 1996 Kingsway's Thankyou Music

Draw me close to the cross,
to the place of your love,
to the place where you poured out your
    mercy;
where the river of life
that flows from your wounded side
brings refreshing to those who draw near.
Draw me close to your throne
where your majesty is shown,
where the crown of my life I lay down.
Draw me close to your side,
where my heart is satisfied,
draw me close to you, Lord, draw me close.

65
Chris Bowater
© 1990 Sovereign Lifestyle Music

Faithful God, faithful God,
all-sufficient one, I worship you.
Shalom my peace,
my strong deliverer,
I lift you up,
faithful God.

66
Brian Doerksen
© 1989 Mercy/Vineyard Publishing/CopyCare

Faithful One, so unchanging,
Ageless One, you're my rock of peace.
Lord of all, I depend on you,
I call out to you again and again,
I call out to you again and again.

You are my rock in times of trouble,
you lift me up when I fall down.
All through the storm your love is the
    anchor,
my hope is in you alone.

67 David Fellingham
© 1997 Kingsway's Thankyou Music

1. Far above all other loves,
   far beyond all other joys,
   heaven's blessings poured on me,
   by the Holy Spirit's pow'r.

   Love's compelling power draws my heart
   into yours;
   Jesus, how I love you, you're my friend and
   my Lord.
   You have died and risen so what else can I
   say?
   How I love you, Lord,
   love you, Lord.

2. All ambition now has gone,
   pleasing you my only goal;
   motivated by your grace,
   living for eternity.

3. Looking with the eye of faith
   for the day of your return;
   in that day I want to stand
   unashamed before your throne.

68 Graham Kendrick
© 1996 Make Way Music

1. Far and near hear the call,
   worship him, Lord of all;
   families of nations, come,
   celebrate what God has done.

2. Deep and wide is the love
   heaven sent from above;
   God's own Son, for sinners died,
   rose again – he is alive.

   Say it loud, say it strong,
   tell the world what God has done;
   say it loud, praise his name,
   let the earth rejoice –
   for the Lord reigns.

3. At his name, let praise begin;
   oceans roar, nature sing,
   for he comes to judge the earth
   in righteousness and in his truth.

69 Ian Smale
© 1984 Kingsway's Thankyou Music

Father God, I wonder
how I managed to exist
without the knowledge of your
    parenthood
and your loving care.
But now I am your child,
I am adopted in your family
and I can never be alone
'cause, Father God, you're there beside me.

I will sing your praises,
I will sing your praises,
I will sing your praises,
    for evermore.
I will sing your praises,
I will sing your praises,
I will sing your praises,
    for evermore.

70 Bob Fitts
© 1985 Scripture in Song/Integrity Music/Kingsway's
Thankyou Music

Father in heaven, how we love you,
we lift your name in all the earth.
May your kingdom be established in our
    praises
as your people declare your mighty works.
Blessèd be the Lord God Almighty,
who was and is and is to come.
Blessèd be the Lord God Almighty,
who reigns for evermore.

71 David Ruis
© 1992 Mercy/Vineyard Publishing/CopyCare

1. Father of creation,
   unfold your sov'reign plan.
   Raise up a chosen generation
   that will march through the land.
   All of creation is longing
   for your unveiling of pow'r.
   Would you release your anointing,
   O God, let this be the hour.

Continued overleaf

Let your glory fall in this room,
let it go forth from here to the nations.
Let your fragrance rest in this place,
as we gather to seek your face.

2. Ruler of the nations,
the world has yet to see
the full release of your promise,
the church in victory.
Turn to us, Lord, and touch us,
make us strong in your might.
Overcome our weakness,
that we could stand up and fight.

Men	Let your kingdom come.
Women	Let your kingdom come.
Men	Let your will be done.
Women	Let your will be done.
Men	Let us see on earth,
Women	let us see on earth
All	the glory of your Son.

72 Darlene Zschech
© 1995 Darlene Zschech/Hillsongs Publishing/Kingsway's Thankyou Music

Father of life, draw me closer,
Lord, my heart is set on you;
let me run the race of time
with your life enfolding mine
and let the peace of God, let it reign.

O Holy Spirit, Lord, my comfort,
strengthen me, hold my head up high;
and I'll stand upon your truth,
bringing glory unto you,
and let the peace of God, let it reign.

O Lord, I hunger for more of you,
rise up within me,
let me know your truth.
O Holy Spirit, saturate my soul,
and let the life of God
fill me now, let your healing pow'r
bring life and make me whole
and let the peace of God, let it reign.

73 John Gibson and Dave Bankhead
© 1992 Kingsway's Thankyou Music/Word Music. Administered by Copycare.

1. Father, we have received
of the fire of your love and your
compassion;
stir our hearts to believe
that your power in us can move in this
nation
as we raise a standard for your Son.

From neighbours to nations with Jesus,
to the ends of the earth in the name of the
Lord,
our hearts are consumed with a passion
to see Jesus receive his reward.

2. Father, we shall arise,
and reach out for the healing of our
nation;
may each day of our lives
be inspired to fulfil your call and
commission
to disciple ev'ry tribe and tongue.

74 Donna Adkins
© 1976 Maranatha! Music/CopyCare

1. Father, we love you,
we worship and adore you,
glorify your name in all the earth.
Glorify your name,
glorify your name,
glorify your name in all the earth.

2. Jesus, we love you . . .

3. Spirit, we love you . . .

75 John Samuel Bewley Monsell (1811-1875) alt.

1. Fight the good fight with all thy might;
Christ is thy strength, and Christ thy right;
lay hold on life, and it shall be
thy joy and crown eternally.

2. Run the straight race through God's
    good grace,
lift up thine eyes and seek his face;
life with its way before us lies;
Christ is the path, and Christ the prize.

3. Cast care aside, lean on thy guide;
his boundless mercy will provide;
trust, and thy trusting soul shall prove
Christ is its life, and Christ its love.

4. Faint not nor fear, his arms are near;
he changeth not, and thou art dear;
only believe, and thou shalt see
that Christ is all in all to thee.

76 Noel and Tricia Richards
© 1994 Kingsway's Thankyou Music

1. Filled with compassion for all creation,
Jesus came into a world that was lost.
There was but one way that he could
    save us,
only through suffering death on a cross.

*God, you are waiting, your heart is
breaking
for all the people who live on the earth.
Stir us to action, filled with your passion
for all the people who live on the earth.*

2. Great is your passion for all the people
living and dying without knowing you.
Having no saviour, they're lost for ever,
if we don't speak out and lead them to
    you.

3. From ev'ry nation we shall be gathered,
millions redeemed shall be Jesus' reward.
Then he will turn and say to his Father:
'Truly my suffering was worth it all.'

77 Horatius Bonar (1808-1889) alt.

1. Fill thou my life, O Lord my God,
in ev'ry part with praise,
that my whole being may proclaim
thy being and thy ways.

2. Not for the lip of praise alone,
nor e'en the praising heart,
I ask, but for a life made up
of praise in ev'ry part.

3. Praise in the common things of life,
its goings out and in;
praise in each duty and each deed,
however small and mean.

4. Fill ev'ry part of me with praise:
let all my being speak
of thee and of thy love, O Lord,
poor though I be and weak.

5. So shalt thou, Lord, receive from me
the praise and glory due;
and so shall I begin on earth
the song for ever new.

6. So shall each fear, each fret, each care,
be turnèd into song;
and ev'ry winding of the way
the echo shall prolong.

7. So shall no part of day or night
unblest or common be;
but all my life, in ev'ry step,
be fellowship with thee.

78 Ian White
© 1988 Little Misty Music. Administered by Kingsway's
Thankyou Music

1. Focus my eyes on you, O Lord,
focus my eyes on you;
to worship in spirit and in truth,
focus my eyes on you.

2. Turn round my life to you, O Lord,
turn round my life to you;
to know from this night you've made me
    new,
turn round my life to you.

Continued overleaf

3. Fill up my heart with praise, O Lord,
   fill up my heart with praise;
   to speak of your love in ev'ry place,
   fill up my heart with praise.

79
William Walsham How (1823-1897)

1. For all the saints
   who from their labours rest,
   who thee by faith
   before the world confessed,
   thy name, O Jesus,
   be for ever blest.

   Alleluia, alleluia!

2. Thou wast their rock,
   their fortress and their might;
   thou, Lord, their captain
   in the well-fought fight;
   thou in the darkness drear
   their one true light.

3. O may thy soldiers,
   faithful, true and bold,
   fight as the saints
   who nobly fought of old,
   and win, with them,
   the victor's crown of gold.

4. O blest communion!
   fellowship divine!
   we feebly struggle,
   they in glory shine;
   yet all are one in thee,
   for all are thine.

5. And when the strife is fierce,
   the warfare long,
   steals on the ear
   the distant triumph song,
   and hearts are brave again,
   and arms are strong.

6. The golden evening
   brightens in the west;
   soon, soon to faithful
   warriors cometh rest;
   sweet is the calm of
   paradise the blest.

7. But lo! There breaks
   a yet more glorious day;
   the saints triumphant
   rise in bright array:
   the King of glory
   passes on his way.

8. From earth's wide bounds,
   from ocean's farthest coast,
   through gates of pearl
   streams in the countless host,
   singing to Father,
   Son and Holy Ghost.

80
Susie Hare
© 2001 Kevin Mayhew Ltd.

1. For all you have done in our lives, Jesus,
   for all that your love has brought us
       through,
   for all that is past and all that's to come,
   we are so grateful to you.

   So we're giving you our worship
   and we're giving you our hearts
   and we're giving you the love that you first
       gave, Jesus to us.

2. For being our strength in times of
       weakness,
   for being our guide when paths are new,
   for being our rock and being our hope,
   we are so grateful to you.

3. For knowing our lives are in your keeping,
   for knowing your hand in all we do,
   for knowing your peace and knowing
       your grace,
   we are so grateful to you.

For all you have done in our lives Jesus,
for all that your love has brought us
    through,
for all that is past and all that's to come,
we are so grateful to you,
we are so grateful to you,
we are so grateful to you.

81
Martin Leckebusch
© 2001 Kevin Mayhew Ltd.

1. For riches of salvation
   give thanks to the Lord;
   release from condemnation,
   give thanks to the Lord;
   for love which truly frees us
   because the Father sees us
   identified with Jesus -
   give thanks, give thanks to the Lord!

2. For courage and endurance
   give thanks to the Lord;
   the Spirit's reassurance,
   give thanks to the Lord;
   for fatherly correction,
   the call to share perfection,
   the hope of resurrection -
   give thanks, give thanks to the Lord!

3. For life in all its fullness
   give thanks to the Lord;
   for all that leads to wholeness
   give thanks to the Lord;
   he knows our ev'ry feeling
   and speaks in grace, revealing
   his comfort and his healing -
   give thanks, give thanks to the Lord!

4. For justice with compassion
   give thanks to the Lord,
   and freedom from oppression,
   give thanks to the Lord;
   for holiness unending,
   a kingdom still extending,
   all earthly pow'r transcending -
   give thanks, give thanks to the Lord!

82
Graham Kendrick
© 1994 Make Way Music

1. For the joys and for the sorrows,
   the best and worst of times,
   for this moment, for tomorrow,
   for all that lies behind;
   fears that crowd around me,
   for the failure of my plans,
   for the dreams of all I hope to be,
   the truth of what I am:

   For this I have Jesus,
   for this I have Jesus,
   for this I have Jesus,
   I have Jesus.

2. For the tears that flow in secret,
   in the broken times,
   for the moments of elation,
   or the troubled mind;
   for all the disappointments,
   or the sting of old regrets,
   all my prayers and longings,
   that seem unanswered yet:

3. For the weakness of my body,
   the burdens of each day,
   for the nights of doubt and worry
   when sleep has fled away;
   needing reassurance
   and the will to start again,
   a steely-eyed endurance,
   the strength to fight and win:

83
Graham Kendrick
© 1985 Kingsway's Thankyou Music

1. For this purpose Christ was revealed
   to destroy all the works of the evil one.
   Christ in us has overcome,
   so with gladness we sing
   and welcome his kingdom in.

Continued overleaf

Over sin he has conquered,
hallelujah, he has conquered.
Over death victorious,
hallelujah, victorious.
Over sickness he has triumphed,
hallelujah, he has triumphed,
Jesus reigns over all!

2. In the name of Jesus we stand,
   by the power of his blood we now claim
      this ground.
   Satan has no authority here,
   pow'rs of darkness must flee,
   for Christ has the victory.

84 Matt Redman
© 1994 Kingsway's Thankyou Music

1. Friend of sinners, Lord of truth,
   I am falling in love with you.
   Friend of sinners, Lord of truth,
   I have fallen in love with you.

   Jesus, I love your name,
   the name by which we're saved.

2. Friend of sinners, Lord of truth
   I am giving my life to you.
   Friend of sinners, Lord of truth,
   I have given my life to you.

85 Isaac Watts (1674-1748), based on Psalm 117

1. From all that dwell below the skies
   let the Creator's praise arise:
   Alleluia.
   Let the Redeemer's name be sung
   through every land by every tongue.
   Alleluia.

2. Eternal are thy mercies, Lord;
   eternal truth attends thy word:
   Alleluia.
   Thy praise shall sound from shore to shore,
   till suns shall rise and set no more.
   Alleluia.

86 Graham Kendrick
© 1983 Kingsway's Thankyou Music

1. From heav'n you came, helpless babe,
   entered our world, your glory veiled;
   not to be served but to serve,
   and give your life that we might live.

   This is our God, the Servant King,
   he calls us now to follow him,
   to bring our lives as a daily offering
   of worship to the Servant King.

2. There in the garden of tears,
   my heavy load he chose to bear;
   his heart with sorrow was torn.
   'Yet not my will but yours,' he said.

3. Come, see his hands and his feet,
   the scars that speak of sacrifice,
   hands that flung stars into space,
   to cruel nails surrendered.

4. So let us learn how to serve,
   and in our lives enthrone him;
   each other's needs to prefer,
   for it is Christ we're serving.

87 Susie Hare
© 2001 Kevin Mayhew Ltd.

1. From the heights of glory, to a humble
      birth,
   the Lord of heaven came down to earth.
   And the greatest story that is known to man,
   in a stable room began.

   What a gift, what a gift we are given;
   sacrifice of the Father for us.
   What a gift, what a gift we are given;
   King of kings, Lord of lords, Jesus!

2. From a humble stable, to a world of
      shame,
   the friend of sinners, who calls my name
   brought the love of heaven to the hearts
      of men
   and it gave lives hope again.

3. From a life, so perfect, to a cruel cross,
   the world's redemption, the Father's loss;
   and the nails were driven and the blood
      flowed free
   in the hands outstretched for me.

4. From the grave he's risen, ever glorified,
   to take his place at his Father's side;
   and the greatest glory will be ours to own
   when he comes to take us home.

   What a hope, what a hope we are given,
   sacrifice of the Father for us.
   What a song to proclaim: 'He is risen!
   King of kings, Lord of lords, Jesus!
   King of kings, Lord of lords, Jesus!'

He fights for breath, he fights for me,
loosing sinners from the claims of hell;
and with a shout our souls are free -
death defeated by Immanuel!

4. Now he's standing in the place of
      honour,
   crowned with glory on the highest
      throne,
   interceding for his own belovèd
   till his Father calls to bring them home!
   Then the skies will part as the trumpet
      sounds
   hope of heaven or the fear of hell;
   but the Bride will run to her Lover's arms,
   giving glory to Immanuel!

88
Stuart Townend
© 1999 Kingsway's Thankyou Music

1. From the squalor of a borrowed stable,
   by the Spirit and a virgin's faith;
   to the anguish and the shame of scandal
   came the Saviour of the human race!
   But the skies were filled with the praise of
      heav'n,
   shepherds listen as the angels tell
   of the Gift of God come down to man
   at the dawning of Immanuel.

2. King of heaven now the friend of sinners,
   humble servant in the Father's hands,
   filled with power and the Holy Spirit,
   filled with mercy for the broken man.
   Yes, he walked my road and he felt my
      pain,
   joys and sorrows that I know so well;
   yet his righteous steps give me hope again -
   I will follow my Immanuel!

3. Through the kisses of a friend's betrayal,
   he was lifted on a cruel cross;
   he was punished for a world's
      transgressions,
   he was suffering to save the lost.

89
Stuart Townend
© 1998 Kingsway's Thankyou Music

1. Giver of grace, how priceless your love
      for me,
   purer than silver, more costly than gold.
   Giver of life, all that I'll ever need,
   strength for my body and food for my
      soul.

   Oh, you are good, so good to me.
   Yes, you are good, so good to me.
   Oh, you are good, so good to me.
   Yes, you are good, so good to me.

2. Giver of hope, rock of salvation,
   tower of refuge, yet there in my pain.
   Now I'm secure, loved for eternity,
   showered with blessings and lavished
      with grace.

   I've never known a love so perfect in its
      faithfulness;
   it lifts me up to the highest place.
   A glimpse of heaven and a taste of my
      inheritance,
   I know that one day I'll be with you.

90

Henry Smith
© 1978 Integrity's Hosanna! Music/Kingsway's Thankyou Music

Give thanks with a grateful heart.
Give thanks to the Holy One.
Give thanks because he's given
Jesus Christ, his Son.
Give thanks with a grateful heart.
Give thanks to the Holy One.
Give thanks because he's given
Jesus Christ, his Son.

And now let the weak say, 'I am strong',
let the poor say, 'I am rich',
because of what the Lord has done for us.
And now let the weak say, 'I am strong',
let the poor say, 'I am rich',
because of what the Lord has done for us.

91

Taizé Community
© Ateliers et Presses de Taizé

Gloria, gloria in excelsis Deo!
Gloria, gloria, alleluia, alleluia!

92

John Newton (1725-1807)
based on Isaiah 33:20-21, alt.

1. Glorious things of thee are spoken,
   Zion, city of our God;
   he whose word cannot be broken
   formed thee for his own abode.
   On the Rock of Ages founded,
   what can shake thy sure repose?
   With salvation's walls surrounded,
   thou may'st smile at all thy foes.

2. See, the streams of living waters,
   springing from eternal love,
   well supply thy sons and daughters,
   and all fear of want remove.
   Who can faint while such a river
   ever flows their thirst to assuage?
   Grace which, like the Lord, the giver,
   never fails from age to age.

3. Round each habitation hov'ring,
   see the cloud and fire appear
   for a glory and a cov'ring,
   showing that the Lord is near.
   Thus they march, the pillar leading,
   light by night and shade by day;
   daily on the manna feeding
   which he gives them when they pray.

4. Saviour, if of Zion's city
   I through grace a member am,
   let the world deride or pity,
   I will glory in thy name.
   Fading is the worldling's pleasure,
   boasted pomp and empty show;
   solid joys and lasting treasure
   none but Zion's children know.

93

Danny Daniels
© 1987 Mercy/Vineyard Publishing/CopyCare

Glory, glory in the highest;
glory to the Almighty;
glory to the Lamb of God,
and glory to the living Word;
glory to the Lamb!
(Repeat)

I give glory (glory),
glory (glory),
glory, glory to the Lamb!
I give glory (glory),
glory (glory),
glory, glory to the Lamb!
I give glory to the Lamb!

94

Geoff Bullock
© 1992 Word Music/Maranatha! Music/CopyCare

Glory to the King of kings!
Majesty, pow'r and strength
to the Lord of lords!
(Repeat)

1. Holy One, all creation crowns you
   King of kings.
   Holy One, King of kings,
   Lord of lords, Holy One.

2. Jesus, Lord, with eyes unveiled
   we will see your throne.
   Jesus, Prince of Peace,
   Son of God, Emmanuel.

95

Carol Owens
© 1972 Bud John Songs/EMI Christian Music
Publishing/CopyCare

1. God forgave my sin in Jesus' name,
   I've been born again in Jesus' name;
   and in Jesus' name I come to you
   to share his love as he told me to.

   He said: 'Freely, freely you have received,
   freely, freely give;
   go in my name and because you believe,
   others will know that I live.'

2. All pow'r is given in Jesus' name,
   in earth and heav'n in Jesus' name;
   and in Jesus' name I come to you
   to share his pow'r as he told me to.

96

Graham Kendrick
© 1985 Kingsway's Thankyou Music

God is good, we sing and shout it,
God is good, we celebrate.
God is good, no more we doubt it,
God is good, we know it's true.

And when I think of his love for me,
my heart fills with praise
and I feel like dancing.
For in his heart there is room for me
and I run with arms opened wide.

97

Arthur Campbell Ainger, adapted by Michael Forster
This version © 1996 Kevin Mayhew Ltd.

1. God is working his purpose out
   as year succeeds to year.
   God is working his purpose out,
   and the day is drawing near.
   Nearer and nearer draws the time,
   the time that shall surely be,
   when the earth shall be filled
   with the glory of God
   as the waters cover the sea.

2. From the east to the utmost west
   wherever foot has trod,
   through the mouths of his messengers
   echoes forth the voice of God:
   'Listen to me, ye continents,
   ye islands, give ear to me,
   that the earth shall be filled
   with the glory of God
   as the waters cover the sea.'

3. March we forth in the strength of God,
   his banner is unfurled;
   let the light of the gospel shine
   in the darkness of the world:
   strengthen the weary, heal the sick
   and set ev'ry captive free,
   that the earth shall be filled
   with the glory of God
   as the waters cover the sea.

4. All our efforts are nothing worth
   unless God bless the deed;
   vain our hopes for the harvest tide
   till he brings to life the seed.
   Yet ever nearer draws the time,
   the time that shall surely be,
   when the earth shall be filled
   with the glory of God
   as the waters cover the sea.

98

David Fellingham
© 1982 Kingsway's Thankyou Music

God of glory, we exalt your name,
you who reign in majesty.
We lift our hearts to you
and we will worship, praise and magnify
your holy name.

In pow'r resplendent (in pow'r
   resplendent)
you reign in glory (you reign in glory),
eternal King (eternal King),
you reign for ever.

Continued overleaf

Your word is mighty (your word is
  mighty),
releasing captives (releasing captives),
your love is gracious (your love is
  gracious),
you are my God.

99 Simon and Tina Triffitt
© 1994 Christian Life Publications

God of glory, you are worthy,
you ride above the heavens,
you are Lord,
God of fire, my desire
is to be a vessel in this end time move.

Fire of God's glory, fall on me,
burn away the chaff of self
and set me free;
make me pure and holy,
a light for all to see;
fire of God's glory, fall on me.

100 Chris Bowater
© 1990 Sovereign Lifestyle Music Ltd.

God of grace, I turn my face to you,
I cannot hide;
my nakedness, my shame, my guilt,
are all before your eyes.
Strivings and all anguished dreams
in rags lie at my feet;
and only grace provides the way
for me to stand complete.

And your grace
clothes me in righteousness,
and your mercy
covers me in love.
Your life adorns and beautifies,
I stand complete in you.

101 Henry Francis Lyte (1793-1847)
based on Psalm 67, alt.

1. God of mercy, God of grace,
   show the brightness of thy face;
   shine upon us, Saviour, shine,
   fill thy Church with light divine;
   and thy saving health extend
   unto earth's remotest end.

2. Let the people praise thee, Lord;
   be by all that live adored;
   let the nations shout and sing
   glory to their Saviour King;
   at thy feet their tribute pay,
   and thy holy will obey.

3. Let the people praise thee, Lord;
   earth shall then her fruits afford;
   God to us his blessing give,
   we to God devoted live;
   all below, and all above,
   one in joy and light and love.

102 Chris Bowater
© 1999 Sovereign Lifestyle Music Ltd.

1. Greater grace, deeper mercy,
   wider love, higher ways.
   Perfect peace, complete forgiveness,
   it's all found in you,
   it's all found in you.

2. More than hope, full assurance,
   joy that more than satisfies.
   Comfort, strength, pow'r and healing
   it's all found in you,
   it's all found in you.

   It's all found in you, Jesus,
   it's all found in you.
   All I desire and all I require,
   it's all found in you.

   Mercy triumphs over justice,
   judgement is good, mercy is best.
   Where sin abounds,
   grace is more abounding,
   it's all found in you.

103 Noel Richards and Gerald Coates
© 1992 Kingsway's Thankyou Music

1. Great is the darkness that covers the
     earth,
   oppression, injustice and pain.
   Nations are slipping in hopeless despair,
   though many have come in your name.
   Watching while sanity dies,
   touched by the madness and lies.

   Come, Lord Jesus,
   come, Lord Jesus,
   pour out your Spirit, we pray.
   Come, Lord Jesus,
   come, Lord Jesus,
   pour out your Spirit on us today.

2. May now your church rise with power
     and love,
   this glorious gospel proclaim.
   In every nation salvation will come
   to those who believe in your name.
   Help us bring light to this world
   that we might speed your return.

3. Great celebrations on that final day
   when out of the heavens you come.
   Darkness will vanish, all sorrow will end,
   and rulers will bow at your throne.
   Our great commission complete,
   then face to face we shall meet.

104 Steve McEwan
© 1985 Body Songs/CopyCare

   Great is the Lord and most worthy of
     praise,
   the city of our God, the holy place,
   the joy of the whole earth.
   Great is the Lord in whom we have the
     victory.
   He aids us against the enemy,
   we bow down on our knees.

And, Lord, we want to lift your name on
     high,
and, Lord, we want to thank you
for the works you've done in our lives;
and, Lord, we trust in your unfailing love,
for you alone are God eternal,
throughout earth and heaven above.

105 Thomas O. Chisholm
© 1923 Renewal 1951 by Hope Publishing/CopyCare

1. Great is thy faithfulness,
   O God my Father,
   there is no shadow
   of turning with thee;
   thou changest not,
   thy compassions they fail not;
   as thou hast been
   thou for ever wilt be.

   Great is thy faithfulness!
   Great is thy faithfulness!
   Morning by morning
   new mercies I see;
   all I have needed
   thy hand has provided,
   great is thy faithfulness,
   Lord, unto me!

2. Summer and winter,
   and springtime and harvest,
   sun, moon and stars
   in their courses above,
   join with all nature
   in manifold witness
   to thy great faithfulness,
   mercy and love.

3. Pardon for sin
   and a peace that endureth,
   thine own dear presence
   to cheer and to guide;
   strength for today
   and bright hope for tomorrow,
   blessings all mine,
   with ten thousand beside!

106

William Williams (1717-1791)
trans. Peter Williams (1727-1796) and others

1. Guide me, O thou great Redeemer,
pilgrim through this barren land;
I am weak, but thou art mighty,
hold me with thy pow'rful hand:
Bread of Heaven, Bread of Heaven,
feed me till I want no more,
feed me till I want no more.

2. Open now the crystal fountain,
whence the healing stream doth flow;
let the fire and cloudy pillar
lead me all my journey through;
strong deliv'rer, strong deliv'rer,
be thou still my strength and shield,
be thou still my strength and shield.

3. When I tread the verge of Jordan,
bid my anxious fears subside;
death of death, and hell's destruction,
land me safe on Canaan's side;
songs of praises, songs of praises,
I will ever give to thee,
I will ever give to thee.

107

John Bakewell (1721-1819) alt.

1. Hail, thou once despisèd Jesus,
hail, thou Galilean King!
Thou didst suffer to release us;
thou didst free salvation bring.
Hail, thou universal Saviour,
bearer of our sin and shame;
by thy merits we find favour;
life is given through thy name.

2. Paschal Lamb, by God appointed,
all our sins on thee were laid;
by almighty love anointed,
thou hast full atonement made.
All thy people are forgiven
through the virtue of thy blood;
opened is the gate of heaven,
we are reconciled to God.

3. Jesus, hail! enthroned in glory,
there for ever to abide;
all the heav'nly hosts adore thee,
seated at thy Father's side:
there for sinners thou art pleading,
there thou dost our place prepare;
ever for us interceding,
till in glory we appear.

4. Worship, honour, pow'r and blessing,
thou art worthy to receive;
loudest praises, without ceasing,
it is right for us to give:
help, ye bright angelic spirits!
bring your sweetest, noblest lays;
help to sing our Saviour's merits,
help to chant Immanuel's praise.

108

James Montgomery (1771-1854), based on Psalm 72

1. Hail to the Lord's anointed,
great David's greater son!
Hail, in the time appointed,
his reign on earth begun!
He comes to break oppression,
to set the captive free;
to take away transgression,
and rule in equity.

2. He comes with succour speedy
to those who suffer wrong;
to help the poor and needy,
and bid the weak be strong;
to give them songs for sighing,
their darkness turn to light,
whose souls, condemned and dying,
were precious in his sight.

3. He shall come down like showers
upon the fruitful earth,
and love, joy, hope, like flowers,
spring in his path to birth:
before him on the mountains
shall peace the herald go;
and righteousness in fountains
from hill to valley flow.

4. Kings shall fall down before him,
   and gold and incense bring;
   all nations shall adore him,
   his praise all people sing;
   to him shall prayer unceasing
   and daily vows ascend;
   his kingdom still increasing,
   a kingdom without end.

5. O'er ev'ry foe victorious,
   he on his throne shall rest,
   from age to age more glorious,
   all-blessing and all-blest;
   the tide of time shall never
   his covenant remove;
   his name shall stand for ever;
   that name to us is love.

109 William Cowper (1731-1800) based on John 21:16

1. Hark, my soul, it is the Lord;
   'tis thy Saviour, hear his word;
   Jesus speaks, and speaks to thee,
   'Say, poor sinner, lov'st thou me?

2. 'I delivered thee when bound,
   and, when wounded, healed thy wound;
   sought thee wand'ring, set thee right,
   turned thy darkness into light.

3. 'Can a woman's tender care
   cease towards the child she bare?
   yes, she may forgetful be,
   yet will I remember thee.

4. 'Mine is an unchanging love,
   higher than the heights above,
   deeper than the depths beneath,
   free and faithful, strong as death.

5. 'Thou shalt see my glory soon,
   when the work of grace is done;
   partner of my throne shalt be:
   say, poor sinner, lov'st thou me?'

6. Lord, it is my chief complaint
   that my love is weak and faint;
   yet I love thee, and adore;
   O for grace to love thee more!

110 Charles Wesley, George Whitefield, Martin Madan and others

1. Hark, the herald-angels sing
   glory to the new-born King;
   peace on earth and mercy mild,
   God and sinners reconciled:
   joyful, all ye nations rise,
   join the triumph of the skies,
   with the angelic host proclaim,
   'Christ is born in Bethlehem.'

   Hark, the herald-angels sing
   glory to the new-born King.

2. Christ, by highest heav'n adored,
   Christ, the everlasting Lord,
   late in time behold him come,
   offspring of a virgin's womb!
   Veiled in flesh the Godhead see,
   hail the incarnate Deity!
   Pleased as man with us to dwell,
   Jesus, our Emmanuel.

3. Hail, the heav'n-born Prince of Peace!
   Hail, the Sun of Righteousness!
   Light and life to all he brings,
   ris'n with healing in his wings;
   mild he lays his glory by,
   born that we no more may die,
   born to raise us from the earth,
   born to give us second birth.

111 Matt Redman © 1995 Kingsway's Thankyou Music

1. Have you not said
   as we pass through water,
   you will be with us?
   And you have said
   as we walk through fire,
   we will not be burned.

Continued overleaf

We are not afraid,
for you are with us;
we will testify
to the honour of your name.
We are witnesses,
you have shown us,
you are the one who can save.

Fill us up and send us out
in the power of your name.
Fill us up and send us out
in the power of your name.

2. Bring them from the west,
sons and daughters,
call them for your praise.
Gather from the east
all your children,
coming home again.
Bring them from afar,
all the nations,
from the north and south,
drawing all the peoples in.
Corners of the earth,
come to see
there's only one Saviour and King.

112 Steve and Vikki Cook
© 1990 Integrity's Hosanna! Music/People of Destiny
International/ Kingsway's Thankyou Music

1. He has clothed us with his righteousness,
covered us with his great love.
He has showered us with mercy,
and we delight to know the glorious
    favour,
wondrous favour of God.

We rejoice in the grace of God
poured upon our lives,
loving kindness has come to us
because of Jesus Christ.
We rejoice in the grace of God,
our hearts overflow.
What a joy to know the grace of God.

2. He's brought us into his family,
made us heirs with his own Son.
All good things he freely gives us
and we cannot conceive what God's
    preparing,
God's preparing for us.

113 Gerald Coates, Noel Richards and Tricia Richards
© 1993 Kingsway's Thankyou Music

He has risen, he has risen,
he has risen, Jesus is alive.

1. When the life flowed from his body,
seemed like Jesus' mission failed.
But his sacrifice accomplished,
vict'ry over sin and hell.

2. In the grave God did not leave him,
for his body to decay;
raised to life, the great awakening,
Satan's pow'r he overcame.

3. If there were no resurrection,
we ourselves could not be raised;
but the Son of God is living,
so our hope is not in vain.

4. When the Lord rides out of heaven,
mighty angels at his side,
they will sound the final trumpet,
from the grave we shall arise.

5. He has given life immortal,
we shall see him face to face;
through eternity we'll praise him,
Christ the champion of our faith.

114 Twila Paris
© 1985 Straightway/Mountain Spring/EMI
Christian Music Publishing/CopyCare

He is exalted,
the King is exalted on high,
I will praise him.
He is exalted, for ever exalted,
and I will praise his name.

He is the Lord,
for ever his truth shall reign.
Heaven and earth
rejoice in his holy name.
He is exalted,
the King is exalted on high.

115 Graham Kendrick
© 1994 Make Way Music

1. He is here,
   and we have come to worship him,
   in his presence opening
   the treasures of our hearts.
   He is here,
   the centre of our longings,
   all our restless journeyings
   are ended in his peace.

   And God is here with us,
   our Saviour, Jesus;
   his mercy covers us.
   Immanuel is here,
   so tender, so near.
   We welcome you, Immanuel,
   adore you more than words can tell,
   we worship you.
   Immanuel is here,
   he is here.

2. He is here,
   and we have come to worship him,
   in his presence opening
   the treasures of our hearts.
   He is here,
   the One for whom the angels sing.
   Heav'n and earth are touching,
   this is a holy place.

116 Unknown

He is Lord,
he is Lord,
he is risen from the dead and he is Lord.
Ev'ry knee shall bow,
ev'ry tongue confess
that Jesus Christ is Lord.

117 Paul Oakley
© 1997 Kingsway's Thankyou Music

1. Here I am, and I have come
   to thank you Lord, for all you've done:
   thank you, Lord;
   you paid the price at Calvary,
   you shed your blood, you set me free:
   thank you, Lord;
   no greater love was ever shown,
   no better life ever was laid down.

   And I will always love your name;
   and I will always sing your praise;

2. You took my sin, you took my shame,
   you drank my cup, you bore my pain:
   thank you, Lord;
   you broke the curse, you broke the
     chains,
   in victory from death you rose again:
   thank you, Lord;
   and not by works, but by your grace
   you clothe me now in your
     righteousness.

3. You bid me come, you make me whole,
   you give me peace, you restore my soul:
   thank you, Lord;
   you fill me up, and when I'm full
   you give me more till I overflow:
   thank you, Lord;
   you're making me to be like you,
   to do the works of the Father, too.

118 William Rees

1. Here is love vast as the ocean,
   loving kindness as the flood.
   When the Prince of Life, our ransom,
   shed for us his precious blood.
   Who his love will not remember?
   Who can cease to sing his praise?
   He can never be forgotten,
   throughout heav'n's eternal days.

Continued overleaf

2. On the mount of crucifixion
   fountains opened deep and wide;
   through the floodgates of God's mercy
   flowed a vast and gracious tide.
   Grace and love, like mighty rivers,
   poured incessant from above,
   and heaven's peace and perfect justice
   kissed a guilty world in love.

119
Michael Sandeman
© 1997 Kingsway's Thankyou Music

Here is the risen Son
riding out in glory,
radiating light all around.
Here is the Holy Spirit,
poured out for the nations,
glorifying Jesus the Lamb.

We will stand as a people
who are upright and holy,
we will worship the Lord of hosts.
We will watch, we will wait
on the walls of the city,
we will look and see what he will say to us.

Ev'ry knee shall bow before him,
ev'ry tongue confess
that he is King of kings,
Lord of lords, and ruler of the earth.

120
Graham Kendrick
© 1988 Make Way Music

1. He walked where I walk
   (he walked where I walk).
   He stood where I stand
   (he stood where I stand).
   He felt what I feel
   (he felt what I feel).
   He understands
   (he understands).

He knows my frailty
(he knows my frailty),
shared my humanity
(shared my humanity),
tempted in ev'ry way
(tempted in ev'ry way),
yet without sin
(yet without sin).

God with us, so close to us,
God with us, Immanuel.

2. One of a hated race
   (one of a hated race),
   stung by the prejudice
   (stung by the prejudice),
   suff'ring injustice
   (suff'ring injustice),
   yet he forgives
   (yet he forgives).
   Wept for my wasted years
   (wept for my wasted years),
   paid for my wickedness
   (paid for my wickedness),
   he died in my place
   (he died in my place),
   that I might live
   (that I might live).

121
Maggi Dawn
© 1987 Kingsway's Thankyou Music

1. He was pierced for our transgressions,
   and bruised for our iniquities;
   and to bring us peace he was punished,
   and by his stripes we are healed.

2. He was led like a lamb to the slaughter,
   although he was innocent of crime;
   and cut off from the land of the living,
   he paid for the guilt that was mine.

We like sheep have gone astray,
turned each one to his own way,
and the Lord has laid on him
the iniquity of us all.

122

Jon Mohr
© 1987 Birdwing Music/EMI Christian Music Publishing. Administered by CopyCare Ltd.

He who began a good work in you,
he who began a good work in you
will be faithful to complete it,
he'll be faithful to complete it,
he who started the work
will be faithful to complete it in you.

If the struggle you're facing
is slowly replacing your hope with
   despair,
or the process is long,
and you're losing your song in the night,
you can be sure that the Lord
has his hand on you, safe and secure,
he will never abandon you.
You are his treasure,
and he finds his pleasure in you.

123

Noel and Tricia Richards
© 1996 Kingsway's Thankyou Music

Hold me closer to you each day;
may my love for you never fade.
Keep my focus on all that's true;
may I never lose sight of you.

1. In my failure, in my success,
   if in sadness or happiness,
   be the hope I am clinging to,
   for my heart belongs to you.

2. You are only a breath away,
   watching over me ev'ry day;
   in my heart I am filled with peace
   when I hear you speak to me.

3. No one loves me in the way you do,
   no one cares for me like you do.
   Feels like heaven has broken through;
   God, you know how I love you.

124

Danny Daniels
© 1989 Mercy/Vineyard Publishing/CopyCare

1. Holiness unto the Lord,
   unto the King.
   Holiness unto your name
   I will sing.

   Holiness unto Jesus,
   holiness unto you, Lord.
   Holiness unto Jesus,
   holiness unto you, Lord.

2. I love you, I love your ways,
   I love your name.
   I love you, and all my days
   I'll proclaim:

125

Unknown

1. Holy, holy, holy is the Lord,
   holy is the Lord God almighty.
   Holy, holy, holy is the Lord,
   holy is the Lord God almighty:
   who was, and is, and is to come;
   holy, holy, holy is the Lord.

2. Jesus, Jesus, Jesus is the Lord,
   Jesus is the Lord God almighty.
   Jesus, Jesus, Jesus is the Lord,
   Jesus is the Lord God almighty:
   who was, and is, and is to come;
   Jesus, Jesus, Jesus is the Lord.

3. Worthy, worthy, worthy is the Lord,
   worthy is the Lord God almighty.
   Worthy, worthy, worthy is the Lord,
   worthy is the Lord God almighty:
   who was, and is, and is to come;
   worthy, worthy, worthy is the Lord.

4. Glory, glory, glory to the Lord,
   glory to the Lord God almighty.
   Glory, glory, glory to the Lord,
   glory to the Lord God almighty:
   who was, and is and is to come;
   glory, glory, glory to the Lord.

126
Reginald Heber (1783-1826)

1. Holy, holy, holy, Lord God almighty!
   Early in the morning our song shall rise
      to thee;
   only thou art holy, merciful and mighty,
   God in three persons, blessèd Trinity!

2. Holy, holy, holy! All the saints adore thee,
   casting down their golden crowns
   around the glassy sea;
   cherubim and seraphim falling down
      before thee,
   who were, and are, and evermore shall
      be.

3. Holy, holy, holy! Though the darkness
      hide thee,
   though the sinful mortal eye
      thy glory may not see,
   only thou art holy, there is none beside
      thee,
   perfect in power, in love and purity.

4. Holy, holy, holy, Lord God almighty!
   All thy works shall praise thy name,
   in earth, and sky and sea;
   Holy, holy, holy, Merciful and mighty,
   God in three persons, blessèd Trinity!

127
Carl Tuttle
© Mercy/Vineyard Publishing/CopyCare

1. Hosanna, hosanna, hosanna in the
      highest!
   Hosanna, hosanna, hosanna in the
      highest!
   Lord, we lift up your name,
   with hearts full of praise;
   be exalted, O Lord, my God!
   Hosanna in the highest!

2. Glory, glory, glory to the King of kings!
   Glory, glory, glory to the King of kings!
   Lord, we lift up your name,
   with hearts full of praise;
   be exalted, O Lord, my God!
   Glory to the King of kings!

128
Graham Kendrick and Steve Thompson
© 1991 Make Way Music

1. How can I be free from sin?
   Lead me to the cross of Jesus,
   from the guilt, the pow'r, the pain,
   lead me to the cross of Jesus.

   There's no other way,
   no price that I could pay,
   simply to the cross I cling.
   This is all I need,
   this is all I plead,
   that his blood was shed for me.

2. How can I know peace within?
   Lead me to the cross of Jesus,
   sing a song of joy again,
   lead me to the cross of Jesus.

   Flowing from above,
   all-forgiving love,
   from the Father's heart to me.
   What a gift of grace,
   his own righteousness,
   clothing me in purity.

3. How can I live day by day?
   Lead me to the cross of Jesus,
   following his narrow way,
   lead me to the cross of Jesus.

129
Stuart Townend
© 1995 Kingsway's Thankyou Music

1. How deep the Father's love for us,
   how vast beyond all measure,
   that he should give his only Son
   to make a wretch his treasure.
   How great the pain of searing loss,
   the Father turns his face away,
   as wounds which mar the Chosen One
   bring many sons to glory.

2. Behold the man upon a cross,
my sin upon his shoulders;
ashamed, I hear my mocking voice
call out among the scoffers.
It was my sin that held him there
until it was accomplished;
his dying breath has brought me life –
I know that it is finished.

3. I will not boast in anything,
no gifts, no pow'r, no wisdom;
but I will boast in Jesus Christ,
his death and resurrection.
Why should I gain from his reward?
I cannot give an answer,
but this I know with all my heart,
his wounds have paid my ransom.

130 Joseph Hart (1712-1768)

1. How good is the God we adore!
Our faithful, unchangeable friend:
his love is as great as his pow'r
and knows neither measure nor end.

2. For Christ is the first and the last;
his Spirit will guide us safe home;
we'll praise him for all that is past
and trust him for all that's to come.

131 Leonard E. Smith Jnr
© 1974 Kingsway's Thankyou Music

1. How lovely on the mountains
are the feet of him
who brings good news, good news,
proclaiming peace,
announcing news of happiness:
our God reigns, our God reigns,
our God reigns, our God reigns,
our God reigns, our God reigns!

2. You watchmen, lift your voices
joyfully as one,
shout for your King, your King.
See eye to eye
the Lord restoring Zion:
your God reigns, your God reigns!

3. Waste places of Jerusalem,
break forth with joy,
we are redeemed, redeemed.
The Lord has saved
and comforted his people:
your God reigns, your God reigns!

4. Ends of the earth,
see the salvation of your God,
Jesus is Lord, is Lord.
Before the nations
he has bared his holy arm:
your God reigns, your God reigns!

132 John Newton

1. How sweet the name of Jesus sounds
in a believer's ear!
It soothes our sorrows, heals our wounds,
and drives away our fear.

2. It makes the wounded spirit whole,
and calms the troubled breast;
'tis manna to the hungry soul,
and to the weary, rest.

3. Dear name! the rock on which I build,
my shield and hiding-place,
my never-failing treas'ry filled
with boundless stores of grace.

4. Jesus! my Shepherd, Saviour, Friend,
my Prophet, Priest and King,
my Lord, my life, my way, my end,
accept the praise I bring.

5. Weak is the effort of my heart,
and cold my warmest thought;
but when I see thee as thou art,
I'll praise thee as I ought.

Continued overleaf

6. Till then I would thy love proclaim
   with ev'ry fleeting breath;
   and may the music of thy name
   refresh my soul in death.

133
Mark Altrogge
© 1998 PDI Praise

1. How wondrous is your presence, Lord,
   too awesome to behold.
   The seraphim must turn away,
   the angels are not bold.
   For who can bear the brightness of
   your holy dwelling place?
   Yet by the blood that Jesus shed,
   I dare to lift my gaze.

   Your holiness is beautiful, Oh Lord.
   Your holiness is beautiful, my glorious Lord.
   I see you now by faith, but soon, Lord, face
   *   to face.*
   Your holiness is beautiful, my Lord.

2. I long to see your splendour, Lord,
   you've burned it in my heart.
   My hunger won't be satisfied
   to worship from afar.
   Oh cause your face to shine on me
   and take the veil away;
   and then my joy will be complete,
   I'll sing eternal praise.

134
Susie Hare
© 2001 Kevin Mayhew Ltd.

Humble yourselves, humble yourselves
under God's mighty hand.
Humble yourselves, and in due time
you will be lifted up.

Humble yourselves, humble yourselves,
under God's mighty hand,
casting your care fully on him
because he cares for you.

And the God of all grace who called you
to glory eternal in Christ,
when suffering comes will restore you
and make you strong.
To him be the power for ever and ever.
To him be the power for ever. Amen.
(x2)

135
Dave Bilbrough
© 1983 Kingsway's Thankyou Music

I am a new creation,
no more in condemnation,
here in the grace of God I stand.
My heart is overflowing,
my love just keeps on growing,
here in the grace of God I stand.

And I will praise you, Lord,
yes, I will praise you, Lord,
and I will sing of all that you have done.

A joy that knows no limit,
a lightness in my spirit,
here in the grace of God I stand.

136
Susie Hare
© 2001 Kevin Mayhew Ltd.

1. I am learning, Lord, that in your plan for
   me,
   some things won't be quite the same as I
   would have them be;
   I am learning, Lord, your purposes to
   know;
   any hardship you allow
   will help my faith to grow.

   For I can do all things in him who
   *   strengthens me;*
   in the power of Jesus is where my strength
   *   shall be.*
   For I can do all things in him who
   *   strengthens me;*
   in the power of Jesus is where my strength
   *   shall be.*

2. I am learning, Lord, that in your plan for
    me,
  I must learn acceptance of the things that
    are to be;
  I am learning, Lord, whatever life may
    ask
  you will give me strength enough
  to arm me for my task.

3. I am learning, Lord, that in your plan for
    me,
  all that I will ever do should for your
    glory be;
  I am learning, Lord, to put my trust in
    you;
  even when the way is hard,
  your grace will take me through.

137
Marc Nelson
© 1987 Mercy/Vineyard Publishing/CopyCare

I believe in Jesus;
I believe he is the Son of God.
I believe he died and rose again,
I believe he paid for us all.

And I believe he's here now,
(I believe that he's here),
standing in our midst;
here with the power to heal now,
(with the power to heal),
and the grace to forgive.

I believe in you, Lord;
I believe you are the Son of God.
I believe you died and rose again,
I believe you paid for us all.

And I believe you're here now,
(I believe that you're here),
standing in our midst;
here with the power to heal now,
(with the power to heal),
and the grace to forgive.

138
Dave Bilbrough
© 1991 Kingsway's Thankyou Music

I believe there is a God in heav'n
who paid the price for all my sin;
shed his blood to open up the way
for me to walk with him.
Gave his life upon a cross,
took the punishment for us,
offered up himself in love,
Jesus, Jesus.
'It is finished' was his cry;
not even death could now deny
the Son of God exalted high,
Jesus, Jesus, Jesus.

139
William Young Fullerton
© Copyright control (revived 1996)

1. I cannot tell
how he whom angels worship
should stoop to love
the peoples of the earth,
or why as shepherd
he should seek the wand'rer
with his mysterious promise
of new birth.
But this I know,
that he was born of Mary,
when Bethlehem's manger
was his only home,
and that he lived at
Nazareth and laboured,
and so the Saviour,
Saviour of the world, is come.

Continued overleaf

2. I cannot tell
how silently he suffered,
as with his peace
he graced this place of tears,
or how his heart
upon the cross was broken,
the crown of pain
to three and thirty years.
But this I know,
he heals the broken-hearted,
and stays our sin,
and calms our lurking fear,
and lifts the burden
from the heavy laden,
for yet the Saviour,
Saviour of the world, is here.

3. I cannot tell
how he will win the nations,
how he will claim
his earthly heritage,
how satisfy
the needs and aspirations
of east and west,
of sinner and of sage.
But this I know,
all flesh shall see his glory,
and he shall reap
the harvest he has sown,
and some glad day
his sun shall shine in splendour
when he the Saviour,
Saviour of the world, is known.

4. I cannot tell
how all the lands shall worship,
when, at his bidding,
ev'ry storm is stilled,
or who can say
how great the jubilation
when ev'ry heart
with perfect love is filled.

But this I know,
the skies will thrill with rapture,
and myriad, myriad
human voices sing,
and earth to heav'n,
and heav'n to earth, will answer:
'At last the Saviour,
Saviour of the world, is King!'

140 Susie Hare
© 2001 Kevin Mayhew Ltd.

1. I come into your presence, Holy King,
and at your feet, surrender ev'rything;
my pride, in brokenness to you I bring;
reign in me, reign in me.
I come, as clay within the potter's hand,
and though the pain is hard to
    understand,
Lord, break and mould me now as you
    have planned;
come and reign, come and reign in me

Reign in me, Jesus, reign in me.
Reign in me, Jesus, reign in me.

2. I come before your throne of sov'reignty,
and give my life to your authority;
may there be more of you and less of me;
reign in me, reign in me.
I come, with nowhere left to hide my
    face,
to live my life, dependent on the grace
which lifts me up into a higher place;
come and reign, come and reign in me.

3. I come, no longer captive to the fears
that bound my stubborn heart in wasted
    years;
forgiveness washes me in healing tears;
reign in me, reign in me.
I come, with all my hopes and dreams
    laid down;
I seek, no more, ambitions of my own
except to honour you and you alone;
come and reign, come and reign in me.

141

Carl Tuttle
© 1982 Mercy/Vineyard Publishing/CopyCare

1. I give you all the honour
   and praise that's due your name,
   for you are the King of Glory,
   the Creator of all things.

   And I worship you,
   I give my life to you,
   I fall down on my knees.
   Yes, I worship you,
   I give my life to you,
   I fall down on my knees.

2. As your Spirit moves upon me now,
   you meet my deepest need,
   and I lift my hands up to your throne,
   your mercy I've received.

3. You have broken chains that bound me,
   you've set this captive free,
   I will lift my voice to praise your name
   for all eternity.

142

Mark Altrogge
© 1986 People of Destiny International.
Administered by CopyCare

I have a destiny I know I shall fulfil,
I have a destiny in that city on a hill.
I have a destiny and it's not an empty wish,
for I know I was born for such a time as this.

1. Long before the ages you predestined me
   to walk in all the works you have
       prepared for me.
   You've given me a part to play in history
   to help prepare a bride for eternity.

2. I did not choose you but you have
       chosen me
   and appointed me for bearing fruit
       abundantly.
   I know you will complete the work
       begun in me,
   by the pow'r of your Spirit working
       mightily.

143

Horatius Bonar

1. I heard the voice of Jesus say,
   'Come unto me and rest;
   lay down, thou weary one,
   lay down thy head upon my breast.'
   I came to Jesus as I was,
   so weary, worn and sad;
   I found in him a resting-place,
   and he has made me glad.

2. I heard the voice of Jesus say,
   'Behold, I freely give
   the living water, thirsty one;
   stoop down and drink and live.'
   I came to Jesus, and I drank
   of that life-giving stream;
   my thirst was quenched, my soul revived,
   and now I live in him.

3. I heard the voice of Jesus say,
   'I am this dark world's light;
   look unto me, thy morn shall rise,
   and all thy day be bright.'
   I looked to Jesus, and I found
   in him my star, my sun;
   and in that light of life I'll walk
   till trav'lling days are done.

144

Randy and Terry Butler
© 1993 Mercy/Vineyard Publishing/CopyCare

I know a place, a wonderful place,
where accused and condemned
find mercy and grace,
where the wrongs we have done
and the wrongs done to us
were nailed there with him,
there on the cross.

At the cross (at the cross),
he died for our sin.
At the cross (at the cross),
he gave us life again.

145 D. W. Whittle (1840-1901)

1. I know not why God's wondrous grace
   to me has been made known;
   nor why, unworthy as I am,
   he claimed me for his own.

   But 'I know whom I have believed;
   and am persuaded that he is able
   to keep that which I've committed
   unto him against that day'.

2. I know not how this saving faith
   to me he did impart;
   or how believing in his word
   wrought peace upon my heart.

3. I know not how the Spirit moves,
   convincing us of sin;
   revealing Jesus through the word,
   creating faith in him.

4. I know not what of good or ill
   may be reserved for me -
   of weary ways or golden days
   before his face I see.

146 Andre Kempen
© 1989 Kempen Music/Kingsway's Thankyou Music

I lift my hands to the coming King,
to the great 'I Am',
to you I sing,
for you're the One
who reigns within my heart.

And I will serve no foreign god,
or any other treasure;
you are my heart's desire,
Spirit without measure.
Unto your name
I would bring my sacrifice.

147 Rob Hayward
© 1985 Kingsway's Thankyou Music

I'm accepted, I'm forgiven,
I am fathered by the true and living God.
I'm accepted, no condemnation,
I am loved by the true and living God.
There's no guilt or fear as I draw near
to the Saviour and Creator of the world.
There is joy and peace as I release
my worship to you, O Lord.

148 Walter Chalmers Smith

1. Immortal, invisible,
   God only wise,
   in light inaccessible
   hid from our eyes,
   most blessed, most glorious,
   the Ancient of Days,
   almighty, victorious,
   thy great name we praise.

2. Unresting, unhasting,
   and silent as light,
   nor wanting, nor wasting,
   thou rulest in might;
   thy justice like mountains
   high soaring above
   thy clouds which are fountains
   of goodness and love.

3. To all life thou givest,
   to both great and small;
   in all life thou livest,
   the true life of all;
   we blossom and flourish
   as leaves on the tree,
   and wither and perish;
   but naught changeth thee.

4. Great Father of glory,
   pure Father of light,
   thine angels adore thee,
   all veiling their sight;
   all laud we would render,
   O help us to see,
   'tis only the splendour
   of light hideth thee.

5. Immortal, invisible,
   God only wise,
   in light inaccessible
   hid from our eyes,
   most blessed, most glorious,
   the Ancient of Days,
   almighty, victorious,
   thy great name we praise.

149 Annie Sherwood Hawks (1835-1918)

1. I need thee ev'ry hour,
   most gracious Lord;
   no tender voice like thine
   can peace afford.

   I need thee, O I need thee!
   Ev'ry hour I need thee;
   O bless me now, my Saviour!
   I come to thee.

2. I need thee ev'ry hour,
   stay thou near by;
   temptations lose their pow'r
   when thou art nigh.

3. I need thee ev'ry hour,
   in joy or pain;
   come quickly and abide,
   or life is vain.

4. I need thee ev'ry hour,
   teach me thy will;
   and thy rich promises
   in me fulfil.

5. I need thee ev'ry hour,
   most Holy One;
   O make me thine indeed,
   thou blessèd Son!

150 David Fellingham © 1994 Kingsway's Thankyou Music

In ev'ry circumstance of life
you are with me, glorious Father.
And I have put my trust in you,
that I may know the glorious hope
to which I'm called.

And by the pow'r that works in me,
you've raised me up and set me free;
and now in ev'ry circumstance
I'll prove your love without a doubt;
your joy shall be my strength,
your joy shall be my strength.

151 Jamie Owens-Collins © 1984 Fairhill Music/CopyCare

1. In heav'nly armour we'll enter the land,
   the battle belongs to the Lord.
   No weapon that's fashioned against us
     will stand,
   the battle belongs to the Lord.

   And we sing glory, honour,
   power and strength to the Lord.
   We sing glory, honour,
   power and strength to the Lord.

2. When the power of darkness comes in
     like a flood,
   the battle belongs to the Lord.
   He'll raise up a standard, the power of his
     blood,
   the battle belongs to the Lord.

3. When your enemy presses in hard,
     do not fear,
   the battle belongs to the Lord.
   Take courage, my friend, your redemption
     is near,
   the battle belongs to the Lord.

152

Anna Laetitia Waring (1820-1910) based on Psalm 23

1. In heav'nly love abiding,
   no change my heart shall fear;
   and safe is such confiding,
   for nothing changes here.
   The storm may roar without me,
   my heart may low be laid,
   but God is round about me,
   and can I be dismayed?

2. Wherever he may guide me,
   no want shall turn me back;
   my Shepherd is beside me,
   and nothing shall I lack.
   His wisdom ever waketh,
   his sight is never dim,
   he knows the way he taketh,
   and I will walk with him.

3. Green pastures are before me,
   which yet I have not seen;
   bright skies will soon be o'er me,
   where the dark clouds have been.
   My hope I cannot measure,
   my path to life is free,
   my Saviour has my treasure,
   and he will walk with me.

153

Christina Georgina Rossetti (1830-1894)

1. In the bleak mid-winter
        frosty wind made moan,
   earth stood hard as iron,
        water like a stone;
   snow had fallen, snow on snow,
        snow on snow,
   in the bleak mid-winter, long ago.

2. Our God, heav'n cannot hold him
        nor earth sustain;
   heav'n and earth shall flee away
        when he comes to reign.
   In the bleak mid-winter
        a stable place sufficed
   the Lord God almighty, Jesus Christ.

3. Enough for him, whom cherubim
   worship night and day,
   a breastful of milk,
   and a mangerful of hay:
   enough for him, whom angels
   fall down before,
   the ox and ass and camel which adore.

4. Angels and archangels
   may have gathered there,
   cherubim and seraphim
   thronged the air;
   but only his mother
   in her maiden bliss
   worshipped the belovèd with a kiss.

5. What can I give him,
   poor as I am?
   If I were a shepherd
   I would bring a lamb;
   if I were a wise man
   I would do my part,
   yet what I can I give him:
   give my heart.

154

Maggi Dawn
© 1993 Kingsway's Thankyou Music

1. Into the darkness of this world,
   into the shadows of the night;
   into this loveless place you came,
   lightened our burdens, eased our pain,
   and made these hearts your home.
   Into the darkness once again,
   O come, Lord Jesus, come.

   Come with your love to make us whole,
   come with your light to lead us on,
   driving the darkness far from our souls:
   O come, Lord Jesus, come.

2. Into the longing of our souls,
   into these heavy hearts of stone,
   shine on us now your piercing light,
   order our lives and souls aright,
   by grace and love unknown,
   until in you our hearts unite,
   O come, Lord Jesus, come.

3. O Holy Child, Emmanuel,
   hope of the ages, God with us,
   visit again this broken place,
   till all the earth declares your praise
   and your great mercies own.
   Now let your love be born in us,
   O come, Lord Jesus, come.

(Final refrain)

Come in your glory, take your place,
Jesus, the name above all names,
we long to see you face to face,
O come, Lord Jesus, come.

155 Gerrit Gustafson
© Integrity's Hosanna! Music

Into your courts we come,
deep in our hearts we long to be
near to the throne of your glory.
As we draw near to you,
know that we're here to do your will,
God how we long to be near to you.

May our prayers be like incense rising up to
*   your throne,*
may our songs be a fragrance unto you;
may our lives be as pleasing off'rings in all
*   that we do.*
God how we long to be near to you,
God how we long to be near to you.

156 Terry MacAlmon
© 1989 Integrity's Hosanna! Music/Kingsway's
Thankyou Music

1. I sing praises to your name, O Lord,
   praises to your name, O Lord,
   for your name is great
   and greatly to be praised.
   (Repeat)

2. I give glory to your name, O Lord,
   glory to your name, O Lord,
   for your name is great
   and greatly to be praised.
   (Repeat)

157 John Wimber
© 1980 Mercy/Vineyard Publishing/CopyCare

Isn't he beautiful, beautiful, isn't he?
Prince of Peace, Son of God, isn't he?
Isn't he wonderful, wonderful, isn't he?
Counsellor, Almighty God, isn't he,
isn't he, isn't he?

Yes, you are beautiful, beautiful, yes, you
   are.
Prince of Peace, Son of God, yes, you are.
Yes, you are wonderful, wonderful, yes,
   you are.
Counsellor, Almighty God, yes, you are,
   yes, you are, yes, you are.

158 Charles H. Gabriel
© The Rodeheaver Company/Word Music/CopyCare

1. I stand amazed in the presence
   of Jesus the Nazarene,
   and wonder how he could love me,
   a sinner, condemned, unclean.

   O, how marvellous! O, how wonderful,
   and my song shall ever be:
   O, how marvellous! O, how wonderful!
   is my Saviour's love for me!

2. For me it was in the garden
   he prayed – 'Not my will, but thine';
   he had no tears for his own griefs,
   but sweat drops of blood for mine.

3. In pity angels beheld him,
   and came from the world of light,
   to comfort him in the sorrows
   he bore for my soul that night.

4. He took my sins and my sorrows,
   he made them his very own;
   he bore the burden to Calvary,
   and suffered, and died alone.

5. When with the ransomed in glory
   his face I at last shall see,
   'twill be my joy through the ages
   to sing of his love for me.

159
Edmund Hamilton Sears (1810-1876) alt.

1. It came upon the midnight clear,
   that glorious song of old,
   from angels bending near the earth
   to touch their harps of gold:
   'Peace on the earth, goodwill to all,
   from heav'ns all gracious King!'
   The world in solemn stillness lay
   to hear the angels sing.

2. Still through the cloven skies they come,
   with peaceful wings unfurled;
   and still their heav'nly music floats
   o'er all the weary world:
   above its sad and lowly plains
   they bend on hov'ring wing;
   and ever o'er its Babel-sounds
   the blessèd angels sing.

3. Yet with the woes of sin and strife
   the world has suffered long;
   beneath the angel-strain have rolled
   two thousand years of wrong;
   and warring humankind hears not
   the love-song which they bring;
   O hush the noise of mortal strife,
   and hear the angels sing!

4. And ye, beneath life's crushing load,
   whose forms are bending low,
   who toil along the climbing way
   with painful steps and slow:
   look now! for glad and golden hours
   come swiftly on the wing;
   O rest beside the weary road,
   and hear the angels sing.

5. For lo, the days are hast'ning on,
   by prophets seen of old,
   when with the ever-circling years
   comes round the age of gold;
   when peace shall over all the earth
   its ancient splendours fling,
   and all the world give back the song
   which now the angels sing.

160
William Walsham How (1823-97)

1. It is a thing most wonderful,
   almost too wonderful to be,
   that God's own Son should come from
       heav'n
   and die to save a child like me.

2. And yet I know that it is true:
   he chose a poor and humble lot,
   and wept and toiled, and mourned and
       died,
   for love of those who loved him not.

3. I sometimes think about the cross,
   and shut my eyes, and try to see
   the cruel nails and crown of thorns,
   and Jesus crucified for me.

4. But even could I see him die,
   I could but see a little part
   of that great love, which, like a fire,
   is always burning in his heart.

5. I cannot tell how he could love
   a child so weak and full of sin;
   his love must be most wonderful,
   if he could die my love to win.

6. It is most wonderful to know
   his love for me so free and sure;
   but 'tis more wonderful to see
   my love for him so faint and poor.

7. And yet I want to love thee, Lord;
   O light the flame within my heart,
   and I will love thee more and more,
   until I see thee as thou art.

161
Pete and Cha'Wright
© Free for Good

It is the Lord, the Lord is here,
his arms outstretched to draw us near.
It is his light, the light of love,
the Spirit's pow'r the heavenly dove.
Rest in his arms, receive his grace
and see the truth in Jesus' face.

It is the Lord,
his peace is here,
his blessings fall
as we draw near.

162
Mary Shekleton (1827-1883)

1. It passeth knowledge, that dear love of
   thine,
   my Saviour, Jesus! yet this soul of mine
   would of thy love, in all its breadth and
   length,
   its height and depth, and everlasting
   strength,
   know more and more.

2. It passeth telling, that dear love of thine,
   my Saviour, Jesus! yet these lips of mine
   would fain proclaim, to sinners, far and
   near,
   a love which can remove all guilty fear,
   and love beget.

3. It passeth praises, that dear love of thine,
   my Saviour, Jesus! yet this heart of mine
   would sing that love, so full, so rich, so
   free,
   which brings a rebel sinner, such as me,
   nigh unto God.

4. O fill me, Saviour, Jesus, with thy love;
   lead, lead me to the living fount above;
   thither may I, in simple faith, draw nigh,
   and never to another fountain fly,
   but unto thee.

5. And then, when Jesus face to face I see,
   when at his lofty throne I bow the knee,
   then of his love, in all its breadth and
   length,
   its height and depth, its everlasting
   strength,
   my soul shall sing.

163
Matt Redman and Martin Smith
© 1995 Kingsway's Thankyou Music

1. It's rising up from coast to coast,
   from north to south, and east to west;
   the cry of hearts that love your name,
   which with one voice we will proclaim.

2. The former things have taken place.
   Can this be the new day of praise?
   A heavenly song that comes to birth,
   and reaches out to all the earth.
   O, let the cry to nations ring,
   that all may come and all may sing:

   'Holy is the Lord.
   Holy is the Lord!'

3. And we have heard the Lion's roar,
   that speaks of heaven's love and power.
   Is this the time, is this the call
   that ushers in your kingdom rule?
   O, let the cry to nations ring,
   that all may come and all may sing:

   'Jesus is alive!
   Jesus is alive!'

164
Michael Christ
© 1985 Mercy/Vineyard Publishing/CopyCare

It's your blood that cleanses me,
it's your blood that gives me life,
it's your blood that took my place
in redeeming sacrifice,
and washes me whiter than the snow,
than the snow.
My Jesus, God's precious sacrifice.

165
Mark Altrogge
© 1982 PDI Music/CopyCare

1. I want to serve the purpose of God
   in my generation.
   I want to serve the purpose of God
   while I am alive.
   I want to give my life for something
   that'll last for ever,
   oh, I delight, I delight to do your will.

Continued overleaf

What is on your heart?
Show me what to do.
Let me know your will
and I will follow you.
   (Repeat)

2. I want to build with silver and gold
   in my generation . . .

3. I want to see the kingdom of God
   in my generation . . .

4. I want to see the Lord come again
   in my generation . . .

166

Brent Chambers
© 1977 Scripture in Song.
Administered by Kingsway's Thankyou Music

I will give thanks to thee,
O Lord, among the peoples,
I will sing praises to thee among the
   nations.
For thy steadfast love is great,
is great to the heavens,
and thy faithfulness, thy faithfulness, to
   the clouds.
Be exalted, O God, above the heavens,
let thy glory be over all the earth!

167

Russell L Lowe
© 1989 Integrity's Hosanna! Music. Administered by
Kingsway's Thankyou Music

I will (*echo) magnify (echo) your name,
   O Lord.
I will (echo) exalt you, (echo) for
   evermore.
For you are King of kings, and Lord of
   lords
and you reign in majesty.
Omnipotent Father, creator of all things.

* *Echo on second time only*

168

Geoff Bullock
© 1995 Word Music/ Maranatha! Music/CopyCare

I will never be the same again,
I can never return,
I've closed the door.
I will walk the path,
I'll run the race
and I will never be the same again.

Fall like fire, soak like rain,
flow like mighty waters again and again:
sweep away the darkness,
burn away the chaff
and let a flame burn
to glorify your name.

There are higher heights,
there are deeper seas:
whatever you need to do,
Lord, do in me;
the glory of God fills my life
and I will never be the same again,
and I will never be the same again.

169

Matt Redman
© 1994 Kingsway's Thankyou Music

1. I will offer up my life
   in spirit and truth,
   pouring out the oil of love
   as my worship to you.
   In surrender I must give
   my ev'ry part;
   Lord, receive the sacrifice
   of a broken heart.

Jesus, what can I give,
what can I bring
to so faithful a friend,
to so loving a King?
Saviour, what can be said,
what can be sung
as a praise of your name
for the things you have done?
O my words could not tell,
not even in part,
of the debt of love that is owed
by this thankful heart.

2. You deserve my every breath
   for you've paid the great cost;
   giving up your life to death,
   even death on a cross.
   You took all my shame away,
   there defeated my sin,
   opened up the gates of heav'n,
   and have beckoned me in.

170
Stuart Townend
© 1997 Kingsway's Thankyou Music

1. I will sing of the Lamb, of the price that
   was paid for me,
   purchased by God, giving all he could
   give!
   Here now I stand in the garments of
   righteousness;
   death has no hold, for in Jesus I live.
   I will sing of his blood that flows for my
   wretchedness,
   wounds that are bared, that I may be
   healed;
   pow'r and compassion, the marks of his
   ministry:
   may they be mine as I harvest his field.

   Oh, I will sing of the Lamb.
   Oh, I will sing of the Lamb.
   My heart fills with wonder, my mouth fills
   with praise!
   Hallelujah, hallelujah.

2. Once I was blind, yet believed I saw
   ev'rything,
   proud in my ways, yet a fool in my part;
   lost and alone in the comp'ny of
   multitudes,
   life in my body, yet death in my heart.

   Oh, I will sing of the Lamb.
   Oh, I will sing of the Lamb.
   Oh, why should the King save a sinner like
   me?
   Hallelujah, hallelujah.

3. What shall I give to the man who gave
   ev'rything,
   humbling himself before all he had
   made?
   Dare I withhold my own life from his
   sov'reignty?
   I shall give all for the sake of his name!

   Oh, I will sing of the Lamb.
   Oh, I will sing of the Lamb.
   I'll sing of his love for the rest of my days!
   Hallelujah, hallelujah.

171
Version 1
Francis Harold Rawley (1854-1952)
© Harper Collins Religious. Administered by CopyCare

1. I will sing the wondrous story
   of the Christ who died for me;
   how he left his home in glory,
   for the cross on Calvary.
   I was lost: but Jesus found me -
   found the sheep that went astray;
   threw his loving arms around me,
   drew me back into his way.

2. I was bruised but Jesus healed me -
   faint was I from many a fall;
   sight was gone, and fears possessed me:
   but he freed me from them all.
   Days of darkness still come o'er me;
   sorrow's paths I often tread:
   but the Saviour still is with me,
   by his hand I'm safely led.

3. He will keep me till the river
   rolls its waters at my feet;
   then he'll bear me safely over,
   where the loved ones I shall meet.
   Yes, I'll sing the wondrous story
   of the Christ who died for me;
   sing it with the saints in glory,
   gathered by the crystal sea.

171

Version 2
Francis Harold Rawley (1854-1952)
© Harper Collins Religious. Administered by CopyCare

1. I will sing the wondrous story
   of the Christ who died for me;
   how he left his home in glory,
   for the cross on Calvary.

   Yes, I'll sing the wondrous story
   of the Christ who died for me;
   sing it with the saints in glory,
   gathered by the crystal sea.

2. I was lost, but Jesus found me -
   found the sheep that went astray;
   threw his loving arms around me,
   drew me back into his way.

3. I was bruised, but Jesus healed me -
   faint was I from many a fall;
   sight was gone, and fears possessed me:
   but he freed me from them all.

4. Days of darkness still come o'er me,
   sorrow's paths I often tread;
   but the Saviour still is with me,
   by his hand I'm safely led.

5. *Instrumental verse and chorus*

6. He will keep me till the river
   rolls its waters at my feet;
   then he'll bear me safely over,
   where the loved ones I shall meet.

172

David Ruis
© 1993 Shade Tree Music/Maranatha!
Music/CopyCare

1. I will worship (I will worship)
   with all of my heart (with all of my
      heart).
   I will praise you (I will praise you)
   with all of my strength (all my strength).
   I will seek you (I will seek you)
   all of my days (all of my days).
   I will follow (I will follow)
   all of your ways (all your ways).

I will give you all my worship,
I will give you all my praise.
You alone I long to worship,
you alone are worthy of my praise.

2. I will bow down (I will bow down),
   hail you as King (hail you as King).
   I will serve you (I will serve you),
   give you ev'rything (give you
      ev'rything).
   I will lift up (I will lift up)
   my eyes to your throne (my eyes to your
      throne).
   I will trust you (I will trust you),
   I will trust you alone (trust in you alone).

173

Michael Frye
© 1999 Vineyard Songs

1. Jesus, be the centre,
   be my source,
   be my light.
   Jesus.

2. Jesus, be the centre,
   be my hope,
   be my song.
   Jesus.

   Be the fire in my heart,
   be the wind in these sails,
   be the reason that I live;
   Jesus, Jesus.

3. Jesus, be my vision,
   be my path,
   be my guide.
   Jesus.

174

From *Lyra Davidica*

1. Jesus Christ is ris'n today, alleluia!
   our triumphant holy day, alleluia!
   who did once, upon the cross, alleluia!
   suffer to redeem our loss, alleluia!

2. Hymns of praise then let us sing, alleluia!
unto Christ, our heav'nly King, alleluia!
who endured the cross and grave, alleluia!
sinners to redeem and save, alleluia!

3. But the pains that he endured, alleluia!
our salvation have procured; alleluia!
now above the sky he's King, alleluia!
where the angels ever sing, alleluia!

175
Matt Redman
© 1995 Kingsway's Thankyou Music

1. Jesus Christ, I think upon your sacrifice,
you became nothing, poured out to
death.
Many times I've wondered at your gift of
life,
and I'm in that place once again.
I'm in that place once again.

And once again I look upon the cross where
you died,
I'm humbled by your mercy and I'm broken
inside.
Once again I thank you,
once again I pour out my life.
Thank you for the cross, thank you for the
cross,
thank you for the cross, my friend.

2. Now you are exalted to the highest place,
King of the heavens, where one day I'll
bow.
But for now, I marvel at this saving grace,
and I'm full of praise once again.
I'm full of praise once again.

176
David Barcham

1. Jesus, come to me
now that I need you,
bring your goodness in,
cleanse my heart anew.

2. Take away my doubt,
take away my fear,
cause my heart to know
that you're ever near.

3. Simply now I cry:
'Lay your hand on me.'
Meet, O Master dear,
ev'ry need in me.

4. Lord, I reach to you,
though my faith is small,
trusting that your love
knows no bounds at all.

5. Jesus, change my ways,
make me hear and see,
teach me deeper things,
show your ways to me.

177
Geoff Bullock
© 1995 Word Music Inc./Maranatha! Music/
CopyCare

1. Jesus, God's righteousness revealed,
the Son of Man, the Son of God,
his kingdom comes.
Jesus, redemption's sacrifice,
now glorified, now justified,
his kingdom comes.

And his kingdom will know no end,
and its glory shall know no bounds,
for the majesty and power
of this kingdom's King has come,
and this kingdom's reign,
and this kingdom's rule,
and this kingdom's power and authority,
Jesus, God's righteousness revealed.

2. Jesus, the expression of God's love,
the grace of God, the word of God,
revealed to us;
Jesus, God's holiness displayed,
now glorified, now justified,
his kingdom comes.

178

Wendy Churchill
© 1982 Word's Spirit of Praise Music/CopyCare

1. Jesus is King and I will extol him,
   give him the glory and honour his name.
   He reigns on high, enthroned in the
   heavens,
   Word of the Father, exalted for us.

2. We have a hope that is steadfast and
   certain,
   gone through the curtain and touching
   the throne.
   We have a Priest who is there interceding,
   pouring his grace on our lives day by day.

3. We come to him, our Priest and Apostle,
   clothed in his glory and bearing his
   name,
   laying our lives with gladness before him;
   filled with his Spirit we worship the
   King.

4. O holy One, our hearts do adore you;
   thrilled with your goodness we give you
   our praise.
   Angels in light with worship surround
   him,
   Jesus, our Saviour, for ever the same.

179

David Mansell
© 1982 Word's Spirit of Praise Music/CopyCare

1. Jesus is Lord! creation's voice proclaims it,
   for by his pow'r each tree and flow'r
   was planned and made.
   Jesus is Lord! the universe declares it,
   sun, moon and stars in heaven
   cry, 'Jesus is Lord!'

   Jesus is Lord! Jesus is Lord!
   Praise him with hallelujahs
   for Jesus is Lord.

2. Jesus is Lord! yet from his throne eternal
   in flesh he came to die in pain
   on Calv'ry's tree.
   Jesus is Lord! from him all life
   proceeding,
   yet gave his life a ransom
   thus setting us free.

3. Jesus is Lord! o'er sin the mighty
   conqu'ror,
   from death he rose, and all his foes
   shall own his name.
   Jesus is Lord! God sent his Holy Spirit
   to show by works of power
   that Jesus is Lord.

180

Philip Lawson Johnston
© 1991 Kingsway's Thankyou Music

1. Jesus is the name we honour;
   Jesus is the name we praise.
   Majestic name above all other names,
   the highest heav'n and earth proclaim
   that Jesus is our God.

   We will glorify,
   we will lift him high,
   we will give him honour and praise.
   We will glorify,
   we will lift him high,
   we will give him honour and praise.

2. Jesus is the name we worship;
   Jesus is the name we trust.
   He is the King above all other kings,
   let all creation stand and sing
   that Jesus is our God.

3. Jesus is the Father's splendour;
   Jesus is the Father's joy.
   He will return to reign in majesty,
   and ev'ry eye at last will see
   that Jesus is our God.

181
David Fellingham
© 1998 Kingsway's Thankyou Music

Jesus, Jesus,
healer, Saviour, strong deliverer,
how I love you,
how I love you.

182
Chris Rolinson
© 1988 Kingsway's Thankyou Music

1. Jesus, King of kings,
   we worship and adore you.
   Jesus, Lord of heav'n and earth,
   we bow down at your feet.
   Father, we bring to you our worship,
   your sov'reign will be done,
   on earth your kingdom come,
   through Jesus Christ, your only Son.

2. Jesus, sovereign Lord,
   we worship and adore you.
   Jesus, name above all names,
   we bow down at your feet.
   Father, we offer you our worship,
   your sov'reign will be done,
   on earth your kingdom come,
   through Jesus Christ, your only Son.

3. Jesus, light of the world,
   we worship and adore you.
   Jesus, Lord Emmanuel,
   we bow down at your feet.
   Father, for your delight we worship,
   your sov'reign will be done,
   on earth your kingdom come,
   through Jesus Christ, your only Son.

183
Dennis Jernigan
© 1991 Shepherd's Heart Music/Sovereign Lifestyle Music

Jesus, Lamb of God, worthy is your name.
Jesus, Lamb of God, worthy is your name.

1. You are my strength when I am weak,
   you are the treasure that I seek,
   you are my all in all.
   Seeking you as a precious jewel,
   Lord, to give up, I'd be a fool.
   You are my all in all.

2. Taking my sin, my cross, my shame,
   rising again I bless your name.
   When I fall down, you pick me up,
   when I am dry, you fill my cup.
   You are my all in all.

184
Paul Oakley
© 1995 Kingsway's Thankyou Music

Jesus, lover of my soul,
all consuming fire is in your gaze.
Jesus, I want you to know
I will follow you all my days.
For no one else in history is like you,
and history itself belongs to you.
Alpha and Omega, you have loved me,
and I will share eternity with you.

It's all about you, Jesus,
and all this is for you,
for your glory and your fame.
It's not about me,
as if you should do things my way;
you alone are God,
and I surrender to your ways.

185
Graham Kendrick
© 1992 Make Way Music

1. Jesus, restore to us again
   the gospel of your holy name,
   that comes with pow'r, not words alone,
   owned, signed and sealed from heaven's
       throne.
   Spirit and word in one agree;
   the promise to the power wed.

   The word is near,
   here in our mouths
   and in our hearts,
   the word of faith;
   proclaim it on the Spirit's breath:
   Jesus.

Continued overleaf

2. Your word, O Lord, eternal stands,
   fixed and unchanging in the heav'ns.
   The Word made flesh, to earth came
      down
   to heal our world with nail-pierced
      hands.
   Among us here you lived and breathed,
   you are the message we received.

   The word is near,
   here in our mouths
   and in our hearts,
   the word of faith;
   proclaim it on the Spirit's breath:
   Jesus.

3. Spirit of truth, lead us, we pray,
   into all truth as we obey.
   And as God's will we gladly choose,
   your ancient pow'r again will prove
   Christ's teaching truly comes from God,
   he is indeed the living Word.

4. Upon the heights of this dark land
   with Moses and Elijah stand.
   Reveal your glory once again,
   show us your face, declare your name.
   Prophets and law, in you, complete
   where promises and power meet.

5. Grant us in this decisive hour
   to know the Scriptures and the pow'r;
   the knowledge in experience proved,
   the pow'r that moves and works by love.
   May words and works join hands as one,
   the word go forth, the Spirit come.

186 Isaac Watts (1674-1748) alt.

Use these words when the tune Truro (Tune 1)
is used.

1. Jesus shall reign where'er the sun
   does his successive journeys run;
   his kingdom stretch from shore to shore,
   till moons shall wax and wane no more.

2. People and realms of ev'ry tongue
   dwell on his love with sweetest song,
   and infant voices shall proclaim
   their early blessings on his name.

3. Blessings abound where'er he reigns:
   the pris'ners leap to lose their chains;
   the weary find eternal rest,
   and all the humble poor are blest.

4. To him shall endless prayer be made,
   and praises throng to crown his head;
   his name like incense shall arise
   with ev'ry morning sacrifice.

5. Let ev'ry creature rise and bring
   peculiar honours to our King;
   angels descend with songs again,
   and earth repeat the loud amen.

186 Isaac Watts (1674-1748)

Use these words when the tune Farringdon
(Tune 2) is used.

1. Jesus shall reign where'er the sun
   doth his successive journeys run;
   his kingdom stretch from shore to shore,
   till suns shall rise and set no more.
   For him shall endless prayer be made,
   and praises throng to crown his head;
   his name like sweet perfume shall rise
   with ev'ry morning sacrifice.

2. People and realms of ev'ry tongue
   dwell on his love with sweetest song;
   and infant voices shall proclaim
   their young hosannas to his name.
   Blessings abound where'er he reigns;
   the pris'ner leaps to lose his chains;
   the weary find eternal rest
   and all the humble poor are blessed.

3. Where he displays his healing pow'r,
   death and the curse are known no more;
   in him the tribes of Adam boast
   more blessings than their father lost.
   Let ev'ry creature rise and bring
   its grateful honours to our King;
   angels descend with songs again
   and earth repeat the loud 'Amen!'
   Let ev'ry creature rise and bring
   its grateful honours to our King;
   angels descend with songs again
   and earth repeat the loud 'Amen!'

187 Chris Bowater
© 1988 Sovereign Lifestyle Music

Jesus shall take the highest honour,
Jesus shall take the highest praise;
let all earth join heav'n in exalting
the name which is above all other
    names.
Let's bow the knee in humble adoration,
for at his name ev'ry knee must bow.
Let ev'ry tongue confess
he is Christ, God's only Son,
Sov'reign Lord, we give you glory now.

For all honour and blessing and power
belongs to you, belongs to you.
All honour and blessing and power
belongs to you, belongs to you,
Lord Jesus Christ, Son of the living God.

188 Fred Chedgey
© 1978 Kingsway's Thankyou Music

Jesus, thank you, Jesus, for all you are to
    me,
for all the things you do.
But I thank you most of all, Lord,
for showing me how much I mean to you.

189 Susie Hare
© 2001 Kevin Mayhew Ltd.

1. Jesus, the Holy One,
   the precious gift of God's own Son.
   Jesus, the Holy One,
   we bow before you now.

   We bow down, we bow down,
   we bow down, before you.
   We now down, we bow down,
   we bow down before you.

2. Jesus, the holy Lamb,
   the sacrifice of God for man.
   Jesus, the Holy Lamb,
   we bow before you now.

3. Jesus, the holy name,
   that takes our sin, that bears our shame.
   Jesus, the Holy name,
   we bow before you now.

190 Charles Wesley

1. Jesus, the name high over all,
   in hell, or earth, or sky;
   angels and mortals prostrate fall,
   and devils fear and fly. *(x2)*

2. Jesus, the name to sinners dear,
   the name to sinners giv'n;
   it scatters all their guilty fear,
   it turns their hell to heav'n. *(x2)*

3. Jesus, the pris'ner's fetters breaks,
   and bruises Satan's head;
   pow'r into strengthless souls he speaks,
   and life into the dead. *(x2)*

4. O, that the world might taste and see
   the riches of his grace!
   The arms of love that compass me,
   hold all the human race. *(x2)*

Continued overleaf

5. His only righteousness I show,
   his saving grace proclaim:
   'tis all my business here below
   to cry: 'Behold the Lamb!' *(x2)*

6. Happy, if with my latest breath
   I may but gasp his name:
   preach him to all, and cry in death:
   'Behold, behold the Lamb!' *(x2)*

191 St Bernard of Clairvaux (1091-1153) tr Edward Caswall (1814-1878)

1. Jesus, the very thought of thee
   with sweetness fills the breast;
   but sweeter far thy face to see,
   and in thy presence rest.

2. No voice can sing, nor heart can frame,
   nor can the mind recall
   a sweeter sound than thy blest name,
   O Saviour of us all!

3. O hope of ev'ry contrite heart,
   O joy of all the meek,
   to those who ask, how kind thou art!
   How good to those who seek!

4. But what to those who find? Ah, this
   nor tongue nor pen can show;
   the love of Jesus, what it is
   none but his loved ones know.

5. Jesus, our only joy be thou,
   as thou our prize wilt be;
   in thee be all our glory now,
   and through eternity.

192 12th Century Latin trans. Ray Palmer (1808-1887)

1. Jesus, thou joy of loving hearts,
   thou fount of life, our lives sustain,
   from the best bliss that earth imparts
   we turn unfilled to thee again.

2. Thy truth unchanged hath ever stood;
   thou savest those that on thee call;
   to them that seek thee thou art good,
   to them that find thee, all in all.

3. We taste thee, O thou living bread,
   and long to feast upon thee still;
   we drink of thee, the fountain-head,
   and thirst our souls from thee to fill.

4. Our restless spirits yearn for thee,
   where'er our changeful lot is cast;
   glad when thy gracious smile we see,
   blessed when our faith can hold thee fast.

5. O Jesus, ever with us stay;
   make all our moments calm and bright;
   chase the dark night of sin away;
   shed o'er the world thy holy light.

193 Martin Leckebusch © 2001 Kevin Mayhew Ltd.

1. Jesus, we have heard your Spirit
   saying we belong to you,
   showing us our need for mercy,
   focusing our hopes anew;
   you have won our hearts' devotion,
   now we feel your guiding hand:
   where you lead us, we will follow
   on the paths your love has planned.

2. As a chosen, pilgrim people
   we are learning day by day
   what it means to be disciples,
   to believe and to obey.
   Word and table show your purpose;
   hearts and lives we gladly bring -
   where you lead us, we will follow,
   suff'ring Saviour, risen King.

3. How we yearn that ev'ry people
   should exalt your matchless name,
   yet so often this world's systems
   countermand your regal claim.
   If we stand for truth and justice
   we, like you, may suffer loss;
   where you lead us, we will follow -
   give us grace to bear our cross.

4. So we journey on together,
   keen to make our calling sure;
   through our joys, our fears, our crises,
   may our faith be made mature.
   Jesus, hope of hearts and nations,
   sov'reign Lord of time and space,
   where you lead us, we will follow
   till we see you face to face.

194
Tanya Riches
© 1995 Tanya Riches/Hillsongs Publishing/Kingsway's Thankyou Music

1. Jesus, what a beautiful name.
   Son of God, Son of Man,
   Lamb that was slain.
   Joy and peace, strength and hope,
   grace that blows all fear away.
   Jesus, what a beautiful name.

2. Jesus, what a beautiful name.
   Truth revealed, my future sealed,
   healed my pain.
   Love and freedom, life and warmth,
   grace that blows all fear away.
   Jesus, what a beautiful name.

3. Jesus, what a beautiful name.
   Rescued my soul, my stronghold,
   lifts me from shame.
   Forgiveness, security, power and love,
   grace that blows all fear away.
   Jesus, what a beautiful name.

195
Marilyn Baker
© 1981 Word's Spirit of Praise Music.
Administered bty CopyCare Ltd.

Jesus, you are changing me,
by your Spirit you're making me like you.
Jesus, you're transforming me,
that your loveliness may be seen in all I do.
You are the potter and I am the clay,
help me to be willing to let you have
   your way.
Jesus, you are changing me,
as I let you reign supreme within my heart.

196
Nathan Fellingham
© 1999 Kingsway's Thankyou Music

1. Jesus, you are so precious to me;
   to behold you is all I desire.
   Seated in glory, now and for ever,
   my Jesus, my Saviour, my Lord.

   I worship you,
   I worship you.
   Lord, I worship you,
   yes, I worship you.

2. Jesus, you are so precious to me,
   your beauty has captured my gaze.
   Now I will come and bow down before you,
   and pour sweet perfume on your feet.

197 Isaac Watts (1674-1748)

1. Join all the glorious names
   of wisdom, love, and pow'r,
   that ever mortals knew,
   that angels ever bore:
   all are too mean to speak his worth,
   too mean to set my Saviour forth.

2. Great prophet of my God,
   my tongue would bless thy name:
   by thee the joyful news
   of our salvation came:
   the joyful news of sins forgiv'n,
   of hell subdued and peace with heav'n.

3. Jesus, my great high priest,
   offered his blood, and died;
   my guilty conscience seeks
   no sacrifice beside:
   his pow'rful blood did once atone,
   and now it pleads before the throne.

4. My Saviour and my Lord,
   my conqu'ror and my King,
   thy sceptre and thy sword,
   thy reigning grace I sing:
   Thine is the pow'r; behold, I sit
   in willing bonds beneath thy feet.

Continued overleaf

5. Now let my soul arise,
and tread the tempter down:
my captain leads me forth
to conquest and a crown:
march on, nor fear to win the day,
though death and hell obstruct the way.

6. Should all the hosts of death,
and pow'rs of hell unknown,
put their most dreadful forms
of rage and malice on,
I shall be safe; for Christ displays
superior pow'r and guardian grace.

198 Isaac Watts (1674-1748)

1. Joy to the world! The Lord is come;
let earth receive her King;
let ev'ry heart prepare him room
and heav'n and nature sing,
and heav'n and nature sing,
and heav'n, and heav'n and nature sing.

2. Joy to the earth! The Saviour reigns;
let us our songs employ;
while fields and floods, rocks, hills
and plains
repeat the sounding joy,
repeat the sounding joy,
repeat, repeat the sounding joy.

3. He rules the world with truth and grace,
and makes the nations prove
the glories of his righteousness,
and wonders of his love,
and wonders of his love,
and wonders, wonders of his love.

199 Charlotte Elliott (1789-1871)

1. Just as I am, without one plea
but that thy blood was shed for me,
and that thou bid'st me come to thee,
O Lamb of God, I come.

2. Just as I am, though tossed about
with many a conflict, many a doubt,
fightings and fears within, without,
O Lamb of God, I come.

3. Just as I am, poor, wretched, blind;
sight, riches, healing of the mind,
yea, all I need, in thee to find,
O Lamb of God, I come.

4. Just as I am, thou wilt receive,
wilt welcome, pardon, cleanse, relieve:
because thy promise I believe,
O Lamb of God, I come.

5. Just as I am, thy love unknown
has broken ev'ry barrier down,
now to be thine, yea, thine alone,
O Lamb of God, I come.

6. Just as I am, of that free love
the breadth, length, depth and height
to prove,
here for a season, then above,
O Lamb of God, I come.

200 Chris Bowater
© 1988 Sovereign Lifestyle Music Ltd.

Lamb of God, Holy One,
Jesus Christ, Son of God,
lifted up willingly to die;
that I the guilty one may know
the blood once shed still freely flowing,
still cleansing, still healing.

I exalt you, Jesus, my sacrifice,
I exalt you, my Redeemer and my Lord.
I exalt you, worthy Lamb of God,
and in honour I bow down
before your throne.

201 James Edmeston (1791-1867)

1. Lead us, heav'nly Father, lead us
   o'er the world's tempestuous sea;
   guard us, guide us, keep us, feed us,
   for we have no help but thee;
   yet possessing ev'ry blessing
   if our God our Father be.

2. Saviour, breathe forgiveness o'er us:
   all our weakness thou dost know;
   thou didst tread this earth before us,
   thou didst feel its keenest woe;
   lone and dreary, faint and weary,
   through the desert thou didst go.

3. Spirit of our God, descending,
   fill our hearts with heav'nly joy,
   love with every passion blending,
   pleasure that can never cloy:
   thus provided, pardoned, guided,
   nothing can our peace destroy.

202 Matt Redman
© 1997 Kingsway's Thankyou Music

Let ev'rything that, ev'rything that,
ev'rything that has breath,
praise the Lord.
Let ev'rything that, ev'rything that,
ev'rything that has breath,
praise the Lord.

1. Praise you in the morning,
   praise you in the ev'ning,
   praise you when I'm young and when I'm
       old.
   Praise you when I'm laughing,
   praise you when I'm grieving,
   praise you ev'ry season of the soul.
   If we could see how much you're worth,
   your pow'r, your might, your endless
       love,
   then surely we would never cease to
       praise.

2. Praise you in the heavens,
   joining with the angels,
   praising you for ever and a day.
   Praise you on the earth now,
   joining with creation,
   calling all the nations to your praise.
   If they could see how much you're worth,
   your pow'r, your might, your endless
       love,
   then surely they would never cease to
       praise.

   Let ev'rything that, ev'rything that,
   ev'rything that has breath, praise the Lord.
   Let ev'rything that, ev'rything that,
   ev'rything that has breath, praise the Lord.

203 Debbye Graafsma
© 1992 WordPsalm Ministries Inc. Administered by
Kingsway's Thankyou Music

Let ev'ry tribe and ev'ry tongue
bring praise to the Lamb,
for he has triumphed over all,
he has triumphed.
With his blood he has redeemed us
for ever to reign with him in glory, amen.

We sing glory, glory to the Lamb;
Son of God, the great I Am.
Awesome in splendour, triumphant king,
we give you praise and dominion over all.

Worthy, worthy is the Lamb;
holy, resurrected Lamb.
Jesus, King Jesus, pre-eminent God,
we give you praise, we give you praise over
all.

204 Mike and Claire McIntosh
© 1982 Mike and Claire McIntosh

1. Let praises ring, let praises ring,
   lift voices up to love him,
   lift hearts and hands to touch him,
   O let praises ring.
   And fill the skies with anthems high
   that tell his excellencies,
   as priests and kings who rule with him
   through all eternity;

Continued overleaf

let praises ring, let praises ring
to our glorious King.

2. Let praises ring, let praises ring,
bow down in adoration,
cry out his exaltation,
O let praises ring.
And lift the name above all names
till ev'ry nation knows
the love of God has come to men,
his mercies overflow.

205 John Milton (1608-1674), based on Psalm 136

1. Let us, with a gladsome mind,
praise the Lord, for he is kind;

   for his mercies ay endure,
   ever faithful, ever sure.

2. Let us blaze his name abroad,
for of gods he is the God;

3, He, with all-commanding might,
filled the new-made world with light;

4. He the golden-tressèd sun
caused all day his course to run;

5. And the moon to shine at night,
'mid her starry sisters bright;

6. All things living he doth feed,
his full hand supplies their need;

7. Let us, with a gladsome mind,
praise the Lord, for he is kind;

206 John Watson
© 1986 Ampelos Music/CopyCare

1. Let your living water flow over my soul.
Let your Holy Spirit come and take
control
of ev'ry situation that has troubled my
mind.
All my cares and burdens on to you I
roll.

Jesus, Jesus, Jesus.
Father, Father, Father.
Spirit, Spirit, Spirit.

2. Come now, Holy Spirit, and take
control.
Hold me in your loving arms and make
me whole.
Wipe away all doubt and fear and take
my pride.
Draw me to your love and keep me by
your side.

3. Give your life to Jesus, let him fill your
soul.
Let him take you in his arms and make
you whole.
As you give your life to him, he'll set you
free.
You will live and reign with him
eternally.

4. Let your living water flow over my soul.
Let your Holy Spirit come and take
control
of ev'ry situation that has troubled my
mind.
All my cares and burdens on to you I
roll.

207 Trevor Burch
© Trevor Burch. Used by permission

1. Lift up your heads,
your king is on his throne;
look with the eyes of faith,
he reigns supreme alone.
Lift up your hearts
and in his presence stand.
He is the King of glory,
Saviour of mankind.

2. Lift up your voice
and let your praises ring;
your Saviour who is worthy,
give him ev'rything.
Lift up your hands,
made holy by the cross,
in joyful, living worship
to the King of kings.

3. Jesus, we are yours,
by your blood made whole;
now accept our worship
from our heart and soul.
Jesus is Lord,
our hearts cry out to you;
majestic in splendour,
holy, just and true.
Jesus is King,
in glad submission bow;
to worship and adore him,
King of glory now.

208 Graham Kendrick
© 1988 Make Way Music

1. Light has dawned that ever shall blaze,
darkness flees away.
Christ the light has shone in our hearts,
turning night to day.

We proclaim him King of kings,
we lift high his name.
Heav'n and earth shall bow at his feet,
when he comes to reign.

(Women)
2. Saviour of the world is he,
heaven's King come down.
Judgement, love and mercy meet
at his thorny crown.

(Men)
3. Life has sprung from hearts of stone,
by the Spirit's breath.
Hell shall let its captives go,
life has conquered death.

4. Blood has flowed that cleanses from sin,
God his love has proved.
Men may mock and demons may rage,
we shall not be moved!

(Refrain twice to end)

209 Charles Wesley, John Cennick and Martin Madan

1. Lo, he comes with clouds descending,
once for mortal sinners slain;
thousand, thousand saints attending
swell the triumph of his train.
Alleluia! Alleluia! Alleluia!
Christ appears on earth to reign.

2. Ev'ry eye shall now behold him
robed in glorious majesty;
we who set at naught and sold him,
pierced and nailed him to the tree,
deeply wailing, deeply wailing, deeply
wailing,
shall the true Messiah see.

3. Those dear tokens of his passion
still his dazzling body bears,
cause of endless exultation
to his ransomed worshippers:
with what rapture, with what rapture,
with what rapture
gaze we on those glorious scars!

4. Yea, amen, let all adore thee,
high on thine eternal throne;
Saviour, take the pow'r and glory,
claim the kingdom for thine own.
Alleluia! Alleluia! Alleluia!
Thou shalt reign, and thou alone.

210 Thomas Kelly (1769-1854)

1. Look, ye saints, the sight is glorious:
see the Man of Sorrows now;
from the fight returned victorious,
ev'ry knee to him shall bow:
Crown him, crown him! *(x2)*
Crowns become the Victor's brow.

Continued overleaf

2. Crown the Saviour! angels, crown him!
   Rich the trophies Jesus brings;
   in the seat of pow'r enthrone him,
   while the vault of heaven rings:
   Crown him, crown him! *(x2)*
   Crown the Saviour King of kings!

3. Sinners in derision crowned him,
   mocking thus the Saviour's claim;
   saints and angels crowd around him,
   own his title, praise his name:
   Crown him, crown him! *(x2)*
   spread abroad the Victor's fame.

4. Hark, those bursts of acclamation!
   Hark those loud triumphant chords!
   Jesus takes the highest station:
   O what joy the sight affords!
   Crown him, crown him! *(x2)*
   King of kings and Lord of lords!

211 George Hugh Bourne (1840-1925)

1. Lord, enthroned in heav'nly splendour,
   first begotten from the dead,
   thou alone, our strong defender,
   liftest up thy people's head.
   Alleluia, alleluia,
   Jesu, true and living bread.

2. Here our humblest homage pay we,
   here in loving rev'rence bow;
   here for faith's discernment pray we,
   lest we fail to know thee now.
   Alleluia, alleluia,
   thou art here, we ask not how.

3. Though the lowliest form doth veil thee
   as of old in Bethlehem,
   here as there thine angels hail thee,
   Branch and Flow'r of Jesse's Stem.
   Alleluia, alleluia,
   we in worship join with them.

4. Paschal Lamb, thine off'ring, finished
   once for all when thou wast slain,
   in its fullness undiminished
   shall for evermore remain.
   Alleluia, alleluia,
   cleansing souls from ev'ry stain.

5. Life-imparting heav'nly manna,
   stricken rock with streaming side,
   heav'n and earth with loud hosanna
   worship thee, the Lamb who died.
   Alleluia, alleluia,
   ris'n, ascended, glorified!

212 Timothy Dudley-Smith
© *Timothy Dudley-Smith*

1. Lord, for the years
   your love has kept and guided,
   urged and inspired us,
   cheered us on our way,
   sought us and saved us,
   pardoned and provided,
   Lord of the years,
   we bring our thanks today.

2. Lord, for that word,
   the word of life which fires us,
   speaks to our hearts
   and sets our souls ablaze,
   teaches and trains,
   rebukes us and inspires us,
   Lord of the word,
   receive your people's praise.

3. Lord, for our land,
   in this our generation,
   spirits oppressed by pleasure,
   wealth and care;
   for young and old,
   for commonwealth and nation,
   Lord of our land,
   be pleased to hear our prayer.

4. Lord, for our world;
   when we disown and doubt him,
   loveless in strength,
   and comfortless in pain;
   hungry and helpless,
   lost indeed without him,
   Lord of the world,
   we pray that Christ may reign.

5. Lord for ourselves;
   in living pow'r remake us,
   self on the cross
   and Christ upon the throne;
   past put behind us,
   for the future take us,
   Lord of our lives,
   to live for Christ alone.

213
Stuart Townend
© 1990 Kingsway's Thankyou Music

1. Lord, how majestic you are,
   my eyes meet your gaze
   and my burden is lifted.
   Your word is a lamp to my feet,
   your hand swift to bless
   and your banner a shield.

   You are my ev'rything,
   you who made earth and sky and sea,
   all that you've placed inside of me
   calls out your name.
   To you I bow,
   the King who commands my ev'ry breath,
   the Man who has conquered sin and death,
   my Lord and my King, my ev'rything!

2. Lord, how resplendent you are,
   when I think of your heavens,
   the work of your fingers -
   what is man, that you are mindful of
     him,
   yet you've crowned him with glory
   and caused him to reign!

214
Robert and Dawn Critchley
© 1989 Kingsway's Thankyou Music

1. Lord, I come before your throne of grace;
   I find rest in your presence
   and fullness of joy.
   In worship and wonder
   I behold your face,
   singing: 'What a faithful God have I'.

   What a faithful God have I,
   what a faithful God;
   what a faithful God have I,
   faithful in ev'ry way.

2. Lord of mercy you have heard my cry;
   through the storm you're the beacon,
   my song in the night.
   In the shelter of your wings,
   hear my heart's reply,
   singing: 'What a faithful God have I'.

3. Lord, all sovereign, granting peace from
     heav'n,
   let me comfort those who suffer
   with the comfort you have giv'n.
   I will tell of your great love
   for as long as I live,
   singing: 'What a faithful God have I'.

215
Geoff Bullock
© 1992 Word Music Inc./Maranatha! Music/
CopyCare

1. Lord, I come to you,
   let my heart be changed, renewed,
   flowing from the grace
   that I found in you.
   And, Lord, I've come to know
   the weaknesses I see in me
   will be stripped away
   by the pow'r of your love.

Continued overleaf

Hold me close,
let your love surround me,
bring me near,
draw me to your side;
and as I wait,
I'll rise up like an eagle,
and I will soar with you;
your Spirit leads me on
in the pow'r of your love.

2. Lord, unveil my eyes,
   let me see you face to face,
   the knowledge of your love
   as you live in me.
   Lord, renew my mind
   as your will unfolds in my life,
   in living ev'ry day
   in the pow'r of your love.

216
Rick Founds
© 1989 Maranatha! Music/CopyCare

Lord, I lift your name on high;
Lord, I love to sing your praises.
I'm so glad you're in my life;
I'm so glad you came to save us.
(Repeat)

You came from heaven to earth
to show the way,
from the earth to the cross,
my debt to pay,
from the cross to the grave,
from the grave to the sky,
Lord, I lift your name on high.

217
Don Moen and Debbye Graafsma
© 1995 Integrity's Hosanna! Music

1. Lord, I stand in the midst of a multitude
   of those from ev'ry tribe and tongue;
   we are your people, redeemed by your
   blood,
   purchased from death by your love.

There are no words good enough to
   thank you,
there are no words to express my praise;
but I will lift up my voice and sing from
   my heart
with all of my strength.

Hallelujah, hallelujah, hallelujah to the
   Lamb;
hallelujah, hallelujah, by the blood of
   Christ we stand.
Ev'ry tongue, ev'ry tribe, ev'ry people, ev'ry
   land;
giving glory, giving honour, giving praise
   unto the Lamb of God.

2. Lord, we stand by grace in your presence,
   cleansed by the blood of the Lamb;
   we are your children, called by your
   name,
   humbly we bow and we pray.
   Release your power to work in us and
   through us,
   till we are changed to be more like you;
   then all the nations will see your glory
   revealed
   and worship you.

Ev'ry knee shall bow;
ev'ry tongue confess that you are Lord of
all.

218
Marilyn Baker
© 1998 Marilyn Baker Music/Kingsway's Thankyou
Music

1. Lord, I want to tell you how much I love
   you;
   your tenderness and mercy have
   overwhelmed my heart.
   Let my whole life be, an overflow of
   worship,
   all I have and all I am I give back, Lord,
   to you.

2. Lord, I want to tell you my heart's desire;
the love you've put within me will burn
with holy fire.
Let my actions spring from an overflow
of worship;
all I have and all I am I gladly give back
to you.

219 Patrick Appleford (b. 1925)
© 1960 Josef Weinberger Ltd.

1. Lord Jesus Christ, you have come to us,
you are one with us, Mary's Son.
Cleansing our souls from all their sin,
pouring your love and goodness in,
Jesus, our love for you we sing, living Lord.

2. Lord Jesus Christ, now and ev'ry day
teach us how to pray, Son of God.
You have commanded us to do
this in remembrance, Lord, of you.
Into our lives your pow'r breaks through,
living Lord.

3. Lord Jesus Christ, you have come to us,
born as one of us, Mary's Son.
Led out to die on Calvary,
risen from death to set us free,
living Lord Jesus, help us see
you are Lord.

4. Lord Jesus Christ, I would come to you,
live my life for you, Son of God.
All your commands I know are true,
your many gifts will make me new,
into my life your pow'r breaks through,
living Lord.

220 Jessy Dixon, Randy Scruggs and John Thompson
© 1982 Whole Armor Music and Full Armor
Music/TKO Publishing Ltd.

1. Lord of lords, King of kings,
maker of heaven and earth
and all good things.
We give you glory.
Lord Jehovah, Son of Man,
precious Prince of Peace and the great
'I Am'.
We give you glory.

Glory to God! Glory to God!
Glory to God Almighty in the highest!

2. Lord, you're righteous in all your ways.
We bless your holy name
and we will give you praise.
We give you glory.
You reign for ever in majesty.
We praise you and lift you up for eternity.
We give you glory.

221 Timothy Dudley-Smith
© Timothy Dudley-Smith

1. Lord of the Church, we pray for our
renewing:
Christ over all, our undivided aim.
Fire of the Spirit, burn for our enduing,
wind of the Spirit, fan the living flame!
We turn to Christ amid our fear and
failing,
the will that lacks the courage to be free,
the weary labours, all but unavailing,
to bring us nearer what a Church should be.

2. Lord of the Church, we seek a Father's
blessing,
a true repentance and a faith restored,
a swift obedience and a new possessing,
filled with the Holy Spirit of the Lord!
We turn to Christ from all our restless
striving,
unnumbered voices with a single prayer:
the living water for our souls' reviving,
in Christ to live, and love and serve and
care.

3. Lord of the Church, we long for our
uniting,
true to one calling, by one vision stirred;
one cross proclaiming and one creed reciting,
one in the truth of Jesus and his word!
So lead us on; till toil and trouble ended,
one Church triumphant one new song
shall sing,
to praise his glory, risen and ascended,
Christ over all, the everlasting King!

222
Graham Kendrick
© 1987 Make Way Music

1. Lord, the light of your love is shining,
   in the midst of the darkness, shining;
   Jesus, Light of the World, shine upon us,
   set us free by the truth you now bring us.
   Shine on me, shine on me.

   Shine, Jesus, shine,
   fill this land with the Father's glory;
   blaze, Spirit, blaze,
   set our hearts on fire.
   Flow, river, flow,
   flood the nations with grace and mercy;
   send forth your word, Lord,
   and let there be light.

2. Lord, I come to your awesome presence,
   from the shadows into your radiance;
   by the blood I may enter your brightness,
   search me, try me, consume all my
      darkness.
   Shine on me, shine on me.

3. As we gaze on your kingly brightness,
   so our faces display your likeness,
   ever changing from glory to glory;
   mirrored here may our lives tell your
      story.
   Shine on me, shine on me.

223
Susie Hare
© 2001 Kevin Mayhew Ltd.

1. Lord, what a sacrifice I see
   as I turn my eyes to Calvary;
   there, my sins nailed to a tree,
   a King stands in instead of me.

2. Lord, what a promise of your grace
   as I turn my eyes to seek your face;
   clothed in righteousness, I place
   my sinfulness in your embrace.

The greatest love that I will ever know,
the only love that never lets me go,
streams from a heart that loves so perfectly;
the greatest love of all is yours to me.

3. Lord, what a privilege I own
   to freely come before your throne;
   there, to know and to be known,
   surrendered now to you alone.

224
Judy Pruett
© 1985 Kingsway's Thankyou Music

Lord, you are the author of my life,
you have begun a work in me,
you have predestined me to do your
   perfect will.

And Lord, you are the Lord of all my days,
you are the Lord of all my nights,
you have chosen me to carry forth your
   word.

So Lord, finish in me what you've begun,
guide me by your mighty hand,
Lord; let me trust in you.

And Lord, let me seek your holy face,
may I always walk with you, Lord,
and let your will be done.

225
Martin Smith
© 1992 Kingsway's Thankyou Music

Lord, you have my heart,
and I will search for yours;
Jesus, take my life and lead me on.
Lord, you have my heart,
and I will search for yours;
let me be to you a sacrifice.

And I will praise you, Lord.
(I will praise you, Lord).
And I will sing of love come down.
(I will sing of love come down).
And as you show your face,
(show your face),
we'll see your glory here.

226 Susie Hare
© 2001 Kevin Mayhew Ltd.

1. Lord, your love will always find me,
   even in the deepest place;
   even there your hand will lift me
   up into your heart of grace.
   You have planned and you can see
   all that I will ever be;
   Lord, it is too wonderful for me.

   You are the one I'm trusting now,
   you are the one I'm trusting now,
   you are the one I'm trusting now,
   and ev'rything I need, I find in you.

2. Lord, your love will always find me,
   even on the highest hill;
   on the far side of the ocean,
   there your hand will guide me still.
   You have planned and you can see
   all that I will ever be;
   Lord, it is too wonderful for me.

3. Lord, your love will always find me,
   I cannot escape your gaze;
   you know ev'rything about me,
   all my words and all my ways.
   You have planned and you can see
   all that I will ever be;
   Lord, it is too wonderful for me.

4. Search me Lord and know me fully,
   know my heart and know my mind;
   test the anxious thoughts within me,
   purify the things you find.
   You have planned and you can see
   all that I will ever be;
   Lord, it is too wonderful for me.

227 Frank Houghton
© Frank Houghton/Jubilate Hymns

1. Lord, you were rich beyond all
       splendour,
   yet, for love's sake, became so poor;
   leaving your throne in glad surrender,
   sapphire-paved courts for stable floor:
   Lord, you were rich beyond all splendour,
   yet, for love's sake, became so poor.

2. You are our God beyond all praising,
   yet, for love's sake, became a man;
   stooping so low, but sinners raising
   heav'nwards by your eternal plan:
   you are our God, beyond all praising,
   yet, for love's sake, became a man.

3. Lord, you are love beyond all telling,
   Saviour and King, we worship you;
   Emmanuel, within us dwelling,
   make us and keep us pure and true:
   Lord, you are love beyond all telling,
   Saviour and King, we worship you.

228 Charles Wesley

1. Love divine, all loves excelling,
   joy of heav'n, to earth come down,
   fix in us thy humble dwelling,
   all thy faithful mercies crown.

2. Jesu, thou art all compassion,
   pure unbounded love thou art;
   visit us with thy salvation,
   enter every trembling heart.

3. Breathe, O breathe thy loving Spirit
   into ev'ry troubled breast;
   let us all in thee inherit,
   let us find thy promised rest.

4. Take away the love of sinning,
   Alpha and Omega be;
   end of faith, as its beginning,
   set our hearts at liberty.

Continued overleaf

5. Come, Almighty to deliver,
   let us all thy grace receive;
   suddenly return, and never,
   never more thy temples leave.

6. Thee we would be always blessing,
   serve thee as thy hosts above;
   pray, and praise thee without ceasing,
   glory in thy perfect love.

7. Finish then thy new creation,
   pure and spotless let us be;
   let us see thy great salvation
   perfectly restored in thee.

8. Changed from glory into glory,
   till in heav'n we take our place,
   till we cast our crowns before thee,
   lost in wonder, love, and praise.

229
Noel and Tricia Richards
© 1996 Kingsway's Thankyou Music

1. Love songs from heaven are filling the
   earth,
   bringing great hope to all nations;
   evil has prospered, but truth is alive,
   in this dark world the light still shines.

2. Nothing has silenced this gospel of
   Christ;
   it echoes down through the ages.
   Blood of the martyrs has made your
   church strong,
   in this dark world the light still shines.

   For you we live, and for you we may die,
   through us may Jesus be seen;
   for you alone we will offer our lives,
   in this dark world our light will shine.

3. Let ev'ry nation be filled with your song;
   this is the cry of your people,
   'We will not settle for anything less,
   in this dark world our light must shine.'

230
Jack W. Hayford
© 1976 Rocksmith Music/Leosong Copyright Service

Majesty, worship his majesty,
unto Jesus be glory, honour and praise.
Majesty, kingdom authority
flows from his throne unto his own,
his anthem raise.
So exalt, lift up on high the name of Jesus;
magnify, come glorify Christ Jesus the
   King.
Majesty, worship his majesty,
Jesus who died, now glorified,
King of all kings.

231
Sebastian Temple
© 1967 OCP Publications

1. Make me a channel of your peace.
   Where there is hatred, let me bring your
   love.
   Where there is injury, your pardon, Lord,
   and where there's doubt, true faith in you.

   O Master, grant that I may never seek
   so much to be consoled as to console,
   to be understood, as to understand,
   to be loved, as to love with all my soul.

2. Make me a channel of your peace.
   Where there's despair in life, let me bring
   hope.
   Where there is darkness, only light,
   and where there's sadness, ever joy.

3. Make me a channel of your peace.
   It is in pardoning that we are pardoned,
   in giving of ourselves that we receive,
   and in dying that we're born to eternal
   life.

232
Graham Kendrick
© 1986 Kingsway's Thankyou Music

1. Make way, make way, for Christ the King
   in splendour arrives;
   fling wide the gates and welcome him
   into your lives.

Make way (make way),
make way (make way),
for the King of kings
(for the King of kings);
make way (make way),
make way (make way),
and let his kingdom in!

2. He comes the broken hearts to heal,
   the pris'ners to free;
   the deaf shall hear, the lame shall dance,
   the blind shall see.

3. And those who mourn with heavy hearts,
   who weep and sigh,
   with laughter, joy and royal crown
   he'll beautify.

4. We call you now to worship him
   as Lord of all,
   to have no gods before him,
   their thrones must fall.

233 Philipp Bliss, alt.

1. Man of sorrows! What a name
   for the Son of God who came
   ruined sinners to reclaim!
   Alleluia! What a Saviour!

2. Bearing shame and scoffing rude,
   in my place condemned he stood;
   sealed my pardon with his blood:
   Alleluia! What a Saviour!

3. Guilty, vile and helpless we;
   spotless Lamb of God was he:
   full atonement – can it be?
   Alleluia! What a Saviour!

4. Lifted up was he to die:
   'It is finished!' was his cry;
   now in heav'n exalted high:
   Alleluia! What a Saviour!

5. When he comes, our glorious King,
   all his ransomed home to bring,
   then anew this song we'll sing:
   Alleluia! What a Saviour!

234 Frances Ridley Havergal (1836-1879)

1. Master, speak! Thy servant heareth,
   waiting for thy gracious word,
   longing for thy voice that cheereth;
   Master, let it now be heard.
   I am list'ning, Lord, for thee;
   what hast thou to say to me?

2. Speak to me by name, O Master,
   let me know it is to me;
   speak, that I may follow faster,
   with a step more firm and free,
   where the Shepherd leads the flock
   in the shadow of the Rock.

3. Master, speak! Though least and lowest,
   let me not unheard depart;
   Master, speak! For, O, thou knowest
   all the yearning of my heart,
   knowest all its truest need;
   speak, and make me blest indeed.

4. Master, speak: and make me ready,
   when thy voice is truly heard,
   with obedience glad and steady
   still to follow ev'ry word.
   I am list'ning, Lord, for thee;
   Master, speak! O speak to me!

235 Graham Kendrick
© 1986 Kingsway's Thankyou Music

1. May the fragrance of Jesus fill this place
   (may the fragrance of Jesus fill this place).
   May the fragrance of Jesus fill this place
   (lovely fragrance of Jesus),
   rising from the sacrifice
   of lives laid down in adoration.

2. May the glory of Jesus fill his church
   (may the glory of Jesus fill his church).
   May the glory of Jesus fill his church
   (radiant glory of Jesus),
   shining from our faces
   as we gaze in adoration.

Continued overleaf

3. May the beauty of Jesus fill my life
   (may the beauty of Jesus fill my life).
   May the beauty of Jesus fill my life
   (perfect beauty of Jesus),
   fill my thoughts, my words, my deeds;
   my all I give in adoration.
   Fill my thoughts, my words, my deeds;
   my all I give in adoration.

236 Martin Leckebusch
© 2001 Kevin Mayhew Ltd.

1. May the grace of Christ, our Saviour,
   be our guide in all we do,
   for his willing self-abasement
   shows the pathway to pursue;
   as we give to other people
   may he make us rich indeed,
   bringing to our human frailty
   all the strength he knows we need.

2. May the love of God our Father
   clothe and fill us day by day;
   may compassion be our watchword
   and forgiveness chart our way -
   for to holiness he called us,
   to reflect his purity:
   in our actions may his kindness
   be a light for all to see.

3. May the friendship of God's Spirit
   be a joy for ever near;
   in our times of doubt and trouble
   may his presence banish fear.
   As his comfort makes us stronger,
   glorious freedom may we know;
   by the life of God he brings us,
   more like Jesus may we grow.

*(This text can also be sung in the second
person rather the first:*

> *May the grace of Christ, your Saviour,
> be your guide in all you do . . .*

*Such usage may be suitable for a
commissioning service.)*

237 Katie Barclay Wilkinson (1859-1928)

1. May the mind of Christ my Saviour
   live in me from day to day,
   by his love and pow'r controlling
   all I do and say.

2. May the word of God dwell richly
   in my heart from hour to hour,
   so that all may see I triumph
   only through his pow'r.

3. May the peace of God my Father
   rule my life in ev'rything,
   that I may be calm to comfort
   sick and sorrowing.

4. May the love of Jesus fill me,
   as the waters fill the sea;
   him exalting, self abasing,
   this is victory.

5. May I run the race before me,
   strong and brave to face the foe,
   looking only unto Jesus
   as I onward go.

6. May his beauty rest upon me
   as I seek the lost to win,
   and may they forget the channel,
   seeing only him.

238 Graham Kendrick
© 1986 Kingsway's Thankyou Music

1. Meekness and majesty,
   manhood and deity,
   in perfect harmony,
   the Man who is God.
   Lord of eternity
   dwells in humanity,
   kneels in humility
   and washes our feet.

   *O what a mystery,
   meekness and majesty.
   Bow down and worship
   for this is your God,
   this is your God.*

2. Father's pure radiance,
   perfect in innocence,
   yet learns obedience
   to death on a cross.
   Suffering to give us life,
   conquering through sacrifice,
   and as they crucify
   prays: 'Father, forgive.'

3. Wisdom unsearchable,
   God the invisible,
   love indestructible
   in frailty appears.
   Lord of infinity,
   stooping so tenderly,
   lifts our humanity
   to the heights of his throne.

239 Martin Smith
© 1995 Curious? Music UK/Kingsway's Thankyou Music

1. Men of faith, rise up and sing
   of the great and glorious King.
   You are strong when you feel weak,
   in your brokenness complete.

   Shout to the north and the south,
   sing to the east and the west.
   Jesus is Saviour to all,
   Lord of heaven and earth.

2. Rise up, women of the truth,
   stand and sing to broken hearts.
   Who can know the healing pow'r
   of our awesome King of love?

   We've been through fire,
   we've been through rain,
   we've been refined by the pow'r of his
      name.
   We've fallen deeper in love with you,
   you've burned the truth on our lips.

3. Rise up, church with broken wings,
   fill this place with songs again
   of our God who reigns on high,
   by his grace again we'll fly.

240 Steve and Vikki Cook
© 1991 People of Destiny Internation/Word Music.
Administered by Copycare.

1. Most holy judge,
   I stood before you guilty,
   when you sent Jesus
   to the cross for my sin.
   There your love was revealed,
   your justice vindicated.
   One sacrifice has paid the cost
   for all who trust in Jesus.

   Now I'm justified,
   you declare me righteous,
   justified by the blood of the Lamb.
   Justified, freely by your mercy,
   by faith I stand and I'm justified.

2. I come to you
   and I can call you 'Father',
   there is no fear,
   there is no shame before you.
   For by your gift of grace
   now I am one of your children,
   an heir with those who bear your name
   and share the hope of glory.

241 Cha Wright

Most worthy Lord, to be adored,
I come and worship at your throne.
Most precious King, to you I sing,
and bring my love to you, my love to you
   alone.

I sing alleluia to the Lord most high;
alleluias will I raise.
Most Holy One, to you I come
and give my sacrifice, my sacrifice of
   praise.

242
F. W. Faber (1814-1863)

1. My God, how wonderful thou art,
   thy majesty how bright,
   how beautiful thy mercy-seat,
   in depths of burning light!

2. How dread are thine eternal years,
   O everlasting Lord,
   by prostrate spirits day and night
   incessantly adored!

3. How wonderful, how beautiful,
   the sight of thee must be,
   thine endless wisdom, boundless pow'r,
   and aweful purity!

4. O how I fear thee, living God,
   with deepest, tend'rest fears,
   and worship thee with trembling hope,
   and penitential tears!

5. Yet I may love thee too, O Lord,
   almighty as thou art,
   for thou has stooped to ask of me
   the love of my poor heart.

6. No earthly father loves like thee,
   no mother, e'er so mild,
   bears and forbears as thou hast done
   with me thy sinful child.

7. Father of Jesus, love's reward,
   what rapture will it be,
   prostrate before thy throne to lie,
   and gaze and gaze on thee!

243
Graham Kendrick
© 1991 Make Way Music

1. My heart is full of admiration
   for you, my Lord, my God and King.
   Your excellence, my inspiration,
   your words of grace have made my spirit
   sing.

All the glory, honour and pow'r
belong to you, belong to you.
Jesus, Saviour, anointed One,
I worship you, I worship you.

2. You love what's right and hate what's evil,
   therefore your God sets you on high,
   and on your head pours oil of gladness,
   while fragrance fills your royal palaces.

3. Your throne, O God, will last for ever,
   justice will be your royal decree.
   In majesty, ride out victorious,
   for righteousness, truth and humility.

244
Edward Mote
© Jubilate Hymns

1. My hope is built on nothing less
   than Jesus' blood and righteousness;
   no merit of my own I claim,
   but wholly trust in Jesus' name.

On Christ, the solid rock, I stand -
all other ground is sinking sand.

2. When weary in this earthly race,
   I rest on his unchanging grace;
   in ev'ry wild and stormy gale
   my anchor holds and will not fail.

3. His vow, his covenant and blood
   are my defence against the flood;
   when earthly hopes are swept away
   he will uphold me on that day.

4. When the last trumpet's voice shall sound,
   O may I then in him be found!
   Clothed in his righteousness alone,
   faultless to stand before his throne.

245
William R. Featherston and Adoniram J. Gordon

1. My Jesus, I love thee, I know thou art mine.
   For thee all the follies of sin I resign.
   My gracious Redeemer, my Saviour art
      thou.
   If ever I loved thee, my Jesus, 'tis now.

2. I love thee because thou has first lovèd
   me,
   and purchased my pardon on Calvary's
   tree.
   I love thee for wearing the thorns on thy
   brow.
   If ever I loved thee, my Jesus, 'tis now.

3. In mansions of glory and endless delight,
   I'll ever adore thee in heaven so bright.
   I'll sing with a glittering crown on my
   brow.
   If ever I loved thee, my Jesus, 'tis now.

246 Darlene Zschech
© 1993 Darlene Zschech/Hillsongs Publishing/
Kingsway's Thankyou Music

My Jesus, my Saviour,
Lord, there is none like you.
All of my days
I want to praise
the wonders of your mighty love.
My comfort, my shelter,
tower of refuge and strength,
let ev'ry breath,
all that I am,
never cease to worship you.

Shout to the Lord,
all the earth, let us sing
power and majesty, praise to the King.
Mountains bow down and the seas will
*   roar*
at the sound of your name.
I sing for joy
at the work of your hands.
For ever I'll love you, for ever I'll stand.
Nothing compares to the promise
I have in you.

247 Susie Hare
© 2001 Kevin Mayhew Ltd.

1. My Jesus, nothing I withhold from you
   now;
   take my silver and my gold,
   for all that I have belongs to you,
   all that I am and all I do.
   My Jesus, nothing I withhold from you.

2. My Jesus, ev'rything I yield to you now,
   all my selfish pride revealed,
   for nothing compares with knowing you,
   your love alone can make me new.
   My Jesus, ev'rything I yield to you.

3. My Jesus, let your will be done
   and in me finish what you have begun,
   that my life is purposed now to be
   all that your heart desires to see.
   My Jesus, let your will be done in me.

4. My Jesus, nothing I withhold from you
   now;
   take my silver and my gold,
   for all that I have belongs to you,
   all that I am and all I do.
   My Jesus, nothing I withhold from you.

248 Daniel Gardner
© 1986 Integrity's Hosanna! Music/Kingsway's
Thankyou Music

My life is in you, Lord,
my strength is in you, Lord,
my hope is in you, Lord,
in you, it's in you.
*   (Repeat)*

I will praise you with all of my life,
I will praise you with all of my strength,
with all of my life,
with all of my strength.
All of my hope is in you.

249 Noel and Tricia Richards
© *1991 Kingsway's Thankyou Music*

My lips shall praise you, my great
  Redeemer;
my heart will worship, Almighty Saviour.

1. You take all my guilt away,
   turn the darkest night to brightest day;
   you are the restorer of my soul.

2. Love that conquers ev'ry fear,
   in the midst of trouble you draw near;
   you are the restorer of my soul.

3. You're the source of happiness,
   bringing peace when I am in distress;
   you are the restorer of my soul.

250 Graham Kendrick
© *1989 Make Way Music*

1. My Lord, what love is this,
   that pays so dearly,
   that I, the guilty one,
   may go free!

   Amazing love, O what sacrifice,
   the Son of God, giv'n for me.
   My debt he pays, and my death he dies,
   that I might live,
   that I might live.

2. And so they watched him die,
   despised, rejected;
   but O, the blood he shed
   flowed for me!

3. And now this love of Christ
   shall flow like rivers;
   come, wash your guilt away,
   live again!

251 Samuel Crossman (c. 1624-1683)

1. My song is love unknown,
   my Saviour's love to me;
   love to the loveless shown,
   that they might lovely be.
   O who am I that for my sake
   my Lord should take frail flesh, and die?

2. He came from his blest throne
   salvation to bestow;
   but they made strange, and none
   the longed-for Christ would know.
   But O, my friend, my friend indeed,
   who at my need his life did spend!

3. Sometimes they strew his way,
   and his sweet praises sing;
   resounding all the day
   hosannas to their King;
   then 'Crucify!' is all their breath,
   and for his death they thirst and cry.

4. Why, what hath my Lord done?
   What makes this rage and spite?
   He made the lame to run,
   he gave the blind their sight.
   Sweet injuries! Yet they at these
   themselves displease,
     and 'gainst him rise.

5. They rise, and needs will have
   my dear Lord made away;
   a murderer they save,
   the Prince of Life they slay.
   Yet cheerful he to suff'ring goes,
   that he his foes from thence might free.

6. Here might I stay and sing,
   no story so divine;
   never was love, dear King,
   never was grief like thine.
   This is my friend in whose sweet praise
   I all my days could gladly spend.

252 Timothy Dudley-Smith
© *Timothy Dudley-Smith*

1. Name of all majesty,
   fathomless mystery,
   King of the ages
   by angels adored;
   pow'r and authority,
   splendour and dignity,
   bow to his mastery,
   Jesus is Lord!

2. Child of our destiny,
   God from eternity,
   love of the Father
   on sinners outpoured;
   see now what God has done
   sending his only Son,
   Christ the beloved One,
   Jesus is Lord!

3. Saviour of Calvary,
   costliest victory,
   darkness defeated
   and Eden restored;
   born as a man to die,
   nailed to a cross on high,
   cold in the grave to lie,
   Jesus is Lord!

4. Source of all sov'reignty,
   light, immortality,
   life everlasting
   and heaven assured;
   so with the ransomed, we
   praise him eternally,
   Christ in his majesty,
   Jesus is Lord!

253 Mark Altrogge
© *1990 Integrity's Hosanna! Music/PDI Music.*
Administered by Kingsway's Thankyou Music

1. No eye has seen and no ear has heard
   and no mind has ever conceived
   the glorious things that you have prepared
   for ev'ryone who has believed.
   You brought us near, and you called us
      your own,
   and made us joint heirs with your Son.

How high and how wide,
how deep and how long,
how sweet and how strong is your love.
How lavish your grace,
how faithful your ways,
how great is your love, O Lord.

2. Objects of mercy who should have
      known wrath,
   we're filled with unspeakable joy,
   riches of wisdom, unsearchable wealth
   and the wonder of knowing your voice.
   You are our treasure and our great
      reward,
   our hope and our glorious King.

254 Susie Hare
© *2001 Kevin Mayhew Ltd.*

1. No gift so wonderful,
   no love so beautiful,
   in just a humble birth,
   heaven came down to earth.
   And in the still of night,
   the world was given light,
   as into sin and shame,
   the love of heaven came.

Have we any room for Jesus?
Have we any time to spare?
If we turned our eyes,
maybe we'd recognise that he is there.
Have we any room for Jesus?
Have we any time for him?
Are we on our own
or could we give a home to Christ the King?

2. No gift so wonderful,
   no love so beautiful;
   what are we meant to see -
   is it just history?
   And is he still, we find,
   a baby in our mind,
   and is the stable scene
   all it will ever mean?

255

Andy Park
© 1988 Mercy/Vineyard Publishing/CopyCare

1. No one but you, Lord,
   can satisfy the longing in my heart.
   Nothing I do, Lord,
   can take the place of drawing near to you.

   Only you can fill my deepest longing,
   only you can breathe in me new life;
   only you can fill my heart with laughter,
   only you can answer my heart's cry.

2. Father, I love you,
   come satisfy the longing in my heart.
   Fill me, overwhelm me,
   until I know your love deep in my heart.

256

Robert Gay
© 1988 Integrity's Hosanna! Music/Kingsway's
Thankyou Music

No other name but the name of Jesus,
no other name but the name of the Lord;
no other name but the name of Jesus
is worthy of glory,
and worthy of honour,
and worthy of power and all praise.
   (Repeat)

His name is exalted far above the earth.
His name is high above the heavens;
his name is exalted far above the earth;
give glory and honour and praise unto his
   name.

257

Graham Kendrick
© 1997 Ascent Music

1. No scenes of stately majesty
   for the King of kings.
   No nights aglow with candle flame
   for the King of love.
   No flags of empire hung in shame
   for Calvary.
   No flow'rs perfumed the lonely way
   that led him to
   a borrowed tomb for Easter Day.

2. No wreaths upon the ground were laid
   for the King of kings.
   Only a crown of thorns remained
   where he gave his love.
   A message scrawled in irony –
   King of the Jews –
   lay trampled where they turned away,
   and no one knew
   that it was the first Easter Day.

3. Yet nature's finest colours blaze
   for the King of kings.
   And stars in jewelled clusters say,
   'Worship heaven's King.'
   Two thousand springtimes more have
      bloomed –
   is that enough?
   Oh, how can I be satisfied
   until he hears
   the whole world sing of Easter love.

4. My prayers shall be a fragrance sweet
   for the King of kings.
   My love the flowers at his feet
   for the King of love.
   My vigil is to watch and pray
   until he comes.
   My highest tribute to obey
   and live to know
   the pow'r of that first Easter Day.

5. I long for scenes of majesty
   for the risen King.
   For nights aglow with candle flame
   for the King of love.
   A nation hushed upon its knees
   at Calvary,
   where all our sins and griefs were nailed
   and hope was born
   of everlasting Easter Day.

258

Noel and Tricia Richards
© 1989 Kingsway's Thankyou Music

*Nothing shall separate us
from the love of God.
Nothing shall separate us
from the love of God.*

1. God did not spare his only Son,
   gave him to save us all.
   Sin's price was met by Jesus' death
   and heaven's mercy falls.

2. Up from the grave Jesus was raised
   to sit at God's right hand;
   pleading our cause in heaven's courts,
   forgiven we can stand.

3. Now by God's grace we have embraced
   a life set free from sin;
   we shall deny all that destroys
   our union with him.

259

Susie Hare
©2001 Kevin Mayhew Ltd.

1. Nothing we have ever done,
   nothing we have said,
   could have raised us up to life;
   sins had made us dead.
   Nothing we have ever earned brings us to
     this place,
   but now God's throne of judgement
   has become his throne of grace.

   *And he has raised us up to the highest place,
   seated in glory with Jesus.
   And he has raised us up to the highest place,
   seated in glory with him.*

2. Nothing we can ever be,
   nothing we can give,
   can redeem us from the life
   that we used to live.
   Futures of eternal wrath we deserve to
     face,
   but now God's throne of judgement
   has become his throne of grace.

3. We have works prepared for us,
   not for our own pride,
   but that he who works in us
   should be glorified.
   Ways of sin and selfishness melt in his
     embrace
   and now God's throne of judgement
   has become his throne of grace.

260

Lex Loizides
© 1999 Kingsway's Thankyou Music

1. No wonder that we sing,
   he's opened up the joys of heaven;
   we're trusting in his perfect righteousness.
   No wonder that we give,
   we've stumbled on the greatest treasure;
   and all our lives are his,
   for he has bought us with his blood.

   *One sufficient sacrifice,
   one God and one mediator,
   once for all he paid the price,
   and we go free!
   One begotten Son of God,
   one way to our home in heaven,
   Jesus Christ my Saviour and my King!*

2. No wonder that we serve,
   he's teaching us to love our neighbour;
   we're going with the grace of God to all.
   No wonder that we pray,
   believing God will save the seeker;
   to all the world we say
   that we are not ashamed of him.

261

Martin Rinkart (1586-1649)
trans. Catherine Winkworth (1827-1878)

1. Now thank we all our God,
   with hearts and hands and voices,
   who wondrous things hath done,
   in whom his world rejoices;
   who from our mother's arms
   hath blessed us on our way
   with countless gifts of love,
   and still is ours today.

Continued overleaf

2. O may this bounteous God
through all our life be near us,
with ever joyful hearts
and blessèd peace to cheer us;
and keep us in his grace,
and guide us when perplexed,
and free us from all ills
in this world and the next.

3. All praise and thanks to God
the Father now be given,
the Son and him who reigns
with them in highest heaven,
the one eternal God,
whom earth and heav'n adore;
for thus it was, is now,
and shall be evermore.

262
Joey Holder
© 1984 Far Lane Music Publishing

Now unto the King eternal,
unto the King immortal,
unto the King invisible,
the only wise God,
the only wise God.
(Repeat)

Unto the King be glory and honour,
unto the King for ever.
Unto the King be glory and honour
for ever and ever, Amen. Amen.

263
Elizabeth Ann Porter Head
© Copyright control

1. O Breath of Life, come sweeping through
us,
revive your Church with life and pow'r;
O Breath of Life, come cleanse, renew us,
and fit your Church to meet this hour.

2. O Breath of Love, come breathe within
us,
renewing thought and will and heart;
come, love of Christ, afresh to win us,
revive your Church in ev'ry part!

3. O Wind of God, come bend us, break us,
till humbly we confess our need;
then, in your tenderness remake us,
revive, restore – for this we plead.

4. Revive us, Lord; is zeal abating
while harvest fields are vast and white?
Revive us, Lord, the world is waiting –
equip your Church to spread the light.

264
Original Latin attributed to John Francis Wade
trans. Frederick Oakeley (1802-80)

1. O come, all ye faithful,
joyful and triumphant,
come ye, O come ye to Bethlehem;
come and behold him,
born the King of angels:

O come, let us adore him, Christ the Lord.

2. True God of true God,
Light of Light eternal,
lo! he abhors not the Virgin's womb;
Son of the Father,
begotten, not created:

3. Sing, choirs of angels,
sing in exultation,
sing, all ye citizens of heav'n above,
glory to God
in the highest:

4. Yea, Lord, we greet thee,
born this happy morning;
Jesus, to thee be glory giv'n,
Word of the Father,
now in flesh appearing:

265
Graham Kendrick
© 1992 Make Way Music

1. O Father of the fatherless,
in whom all families are blessed,
I love the way you father me.
You gave me life, forgave the past,
now in your arms I'm safe at last;
I love the way you father me.

Father me,
for ever you'll father me,
and in your embrace
I'll be for ever secure;
I love the way you father me.
I love the way you father me.

2. When bruised and broken I draw near,
   you hold me close and dry my tears;
   I love the way you father me.
   At last my fearful heart is still,
   surrendered to your perfect will;
   I love the way you father me.

3. If in my foolishness I stray,
   returning empty and ashamed,
   I love the way you father me.
   Exchanging for my wretchedness
   your radiant robes of righteousness,
   I love the way you father me.

4. And when I look into your eyes,
   from deep within my spirit cries,
   I love the way you father me.
   Before such love I stand amazed
   and ever will through endless days;
   I love the way you father me.

266 W. Cowper (1731-1800) alt.
© This version Jubilate Hymns

1. O for a closer walk with God,
   the calm of sins forgiv'n,
   a light to shine upon the road
   that leads at last to heav'n.

2. O gentle messenger, return -
   return, O holy Dove;
   I hate the sins that made you mourn
   and grieved your heart of love.

3. Restore the happiness I knew
   when first I saw the Lord;
   refresh me with the radiant view
   of Jesus and his word!

4. From ev'ry idol I have known
   now set my spirit free;
   O make me worship you alone,
   and reign supreme in me.

5. So shall my walk be close with God,
   my wand'rings be forgiv'n;
   so shall his light mark out the road
   that leads at last to heav'n.

267 Charles Wesley (1707-1788)

1. O for a heart to praise my God,
   a heart from sin set free;
   a heart that always feels thy blood
   so freely shed for me.

2. A heart resigned, submissive, meek,
   my great Redeemer's throne;
   where only Christ is heard to speak,
   where Jesus reigns alone.

3. A humble, lowly, contrite heart,
   believing true, and clean;
   which neither life nor death can part
   from him who dwells within.

4. A heart in ev'ry thought renewed,
   and full of love divine;
   perfect and right, and pure and good:
   a copy, Lord, of thine.

5. Thy nature, gracious Lord, impart,
   come quickly from above;
   write thy new name upon my heart,
   thy new best name of love.

268

Charles Wesley

1. O for a thousand tongues to sing
    my dear Redeemer's praise,
    my dear Redeemer's praise,
    the glories of my God and King,
    the triumphs of his grace.

2. Jesus! the name that charms our fears,
    that bids our sorrows cease,
    that bids our sorrows cease;
    'tis music in the sinner's ears,
    'tis life and health and peace.

3. He breaks the pow'r of cancelled sin,
    he sets the prisoner free,
    he sets the prisoner free;
    his blood can make the foulest clean;
    his blood availed for me.

4. He speaks; and listening to his voice,
    new life the dead receive,
    new life the dead receive,
    the mournful broken hearts rejoice,
    the humble poor believe.

5. Hear him, ye deaf; his praise, ye dumb,
    your loosened tongues employ,
    your loosened tongues employ;
    ye blind, behold your Saviour come;
    and leap, ye lame, for joy!

6. My gracious Master and my God,
    assist me to proclaim,
    assist me to proclaim
    and spread through all the earth abroad
    the honours of thy name.

269

Jamie Owens-Collins
© 1990 Fairhill Music/CopyCare

1. O God, Most High, Almighty King,
    the champion of heaven, Lord of
        ev'rything;
    you've fought, you've won, death's lost its
        sting,
    and standing in your victory we sing.

You have broken the chains
that held our captive souls.
You have broken the chains
and used them on your foes.
All your enemies are bound,
they tremble at the sound of your name;
Jesus, you have broken the chains.

2. The pow'r of hell has been undone,
    captivity held captive by the risen One,
    and in the name of God's great Son,
    we claim the mighty victory you've won.

(Last time)
Jesus, you have broken the chains.
Jesus, you have broken the chains.

270

William Booth
© 1994 Kingsway's Thankyou Music

1. O God of burning, cleansing flame:
    send the fire!
    Your blood-bought gift today we claim:
    send the fire today!
    Look down and see this waiting host,
    and send the promised Holy Ghost;
    we need another Pentecost!
    Send the fire today!
    Send the fire today!

2. God of Elijah, hear our cry:
    send the fire!
    and make us fit to live or die:
    send the fire today!
    To burn up every trace of sin,
    to bring the light and glory in,
    the revolution now begin!
    Send the fire today!
    Send the fire today!

3. It's fire we want, for fire we plead:
    send the fire!
    The fire will meet our ev'ry need:
    send the fire today!
    For strength to always do what's right,
    for grace to conquer in the fight,
    for pow'r to walk the world in white.
    Send the fire today!
    Send the fire today!

4. To make our weak heart strong and
      brave:
   send the fire!
   To live, a dying world to save:
   send the fire today!
   O, see us on your altar lay,
   we give our lives to you today,
   so crown the off'ring now we pray:
   Send the fire today!
   Send the fire today!
   Send the fire today!

271 Philip Doddridge (1702-1751)

1. O happy day, that fixed my choice
   on thee, my Saviour and my God!
   Well may this glowing heart rejoice,
   and tell its raptures all abroad.

   *Happy day! Happy day!
   when Jesus washed my sins away!
   He taught me how to watch and pray,
   and live rejoicing ev'ry day.
   *Happy day! Happy day!
   when Jesus washed my sins away!

2. 'Tis done, the great transaction's done!
   I am my Lord's, and he is mine;
   he drew me, and I followed on,
   charmed to confess the voice divine.

3. Now rest, my long-divided heart,
   fixed on this blissful centre, rest;
   nor ever from thy Lord depart,
   with him of ev'ry good possessed.

4. High heav'n, that heard the solemn vow,
   that vow renewed shall daily hear,
   till in life's latest hour I bow,
   and bless in death a bond so dear.

   Tune 1: Refrain 'O Happy day!'
   *Tune 2: Refrain 'Happy day!'

272 Gerrit Gustafson
© 1990 Intregrity's Hosanna! Music

1. O how I love thy law,
   it is my meditation all of the day;
   filling my mind and heart,
   with its light I will know the way.

   Thy word is a lamp unto my feet,
   and a light unto my path;
   thy word is my bread,
   by thy word shall I live,
   O how I love thy law,
   O how I love thy law.

2. You are the truth and life,
   and I will cling to ev'ry word that you
      say;
   your wisdom is my delight,
   I will walk in your truth each day.

273 John Ernest Bode (1816 -1874)

1. O Jesus, I have promised
   to serve thee to the end;
   be thou for ever near me,
   my Master and my Friend;
   I shall not fear the battle
   if thou art by my side,
   nor wander from the pathway
   if thou wilt be my Guide.

2. O let me feel thee near me:
   the world is ever near;
   I see the sights that dazzle,
   the tempting sounds I hear;
   my foes are ever near me,
   around me and within;
   but, Jesus, draw thou nearer,
   and shield my soul from sin.

Continued overleaf

3. O let me hear thee speaking
in accents clear and still,
above the storms of passion,
the murmurs of self-will;
O speak to reassure me,
to hasten or control;
O speak, and make me listen,
thou Guardian of my soul.

4. O Jesus, thou hast promised,
to all who follow thee,
that where thou art in glory
there shall thy servants be;
and, Jesus, I have promised
to serve thee to the end;
O give me grace to follow
my Master and my Friend.

5. O let me see thy footmarks,
and in them plant mine own;
my hope to follow duly
is in thy strength alone.
O guide me, call me, draw me,
uphold me to the end;
and then in heav'n receive me,
my Saviour and my Friend.

274 Brenton Brown
© 1999 Vineyard Songs

O kneel me down again,
here at your feet;
show me how much you love humility.
O Spirit, be the star that leads me to
the humble heart of love I see in you.

('cos) You are the God of the broken,
the friend of the weak;
you wash the feet of the weary,
embrace the ones in need.
I want to be like you, Jesus,
to have this heart in me.
You are the God of the humble,
you are the humble King.

275 John Wimber
© 1979 Mercy/Vineyard Publishing/CopyCare

1. O let the Son of God enfold you
with his Spirit and his love,
let him fill your heart and satisfy your
soul.
O let him have the things that hold you,
and his Spirit like a dove
will descend upon your life and make you
whole.

Jesus, O Jesus,
come and fill your lambs.
Jesus, O Jesus,
come and fill your lambs.

2. O come and sing this song with gladness
as your hearts are filled with joy,
lift your hands in sweet surrender to his
name.
O give him all your tears and sadness,
give him all your years of pain,
and you'll enter into life in Jesus' name.

276 Phillips Brooks

1. O little town of Bethlehem,
how still we see thee lie!
Above thy deep and dreamless sleep
the silent stars go by.
Yet in thy dark streets shineth
the everlasting light;
the hopes and fears of the all the years
are met in thee tonight.

2. O morning stars, together
proclaim the holy birth,
and praises sing to God the King,
and peace upon the earth.
For Christ is born of Mary;
and, gathered all above,
while mortals sleep, the angels keep
their watch of wond'ring love.

3. How silently, how silently,
the wondrous gift is giv'n!
So God imparts to human hearts
the blessings of his heav'n.
No ear may hear his coming;
but in this world of sin,
where meek souls will receive him, still
the dear Christ enters in.

4. O holy child of Bethlehem,
descend to us, we pray;
cast out our sin, and enter in,
be born in us today.
We hear the Christmas angels
the great glad tidings tell:
O come to us, abide with us,
our Lord Emmanuel.

277 *© Ateliers et Presses de Taizé*
O Lord hear my prayer,
O Lord hear my prayer.
When I call answer me.
O Lord hear my prayer,
O Lord hear my prayer.
Come and listen to me.

278 Karl Boberg trans. Stuart K. Hine
© 1953 Stuart K. Hine/Kingsway's Thankyou Music

1. O Lord, my God, when I, in awesome
wonder,
consider all the works thy hand has
made,
I see the stars, I hear the rolling thunder,
thy pow'r throughout the universe
displayed.

*Then sings my soul, my Saviour God, to
thee:*
how great thou art, how great thou art.
*Then sings my soul, my Saviour God, to
thee:*
how great thou art, how great thou art.

2. When through the woods and forest
glades I wander,
and hear the birds sing sweetly in the
trees;
when I look down from lofty mountain
grandeur,
and hear the brook, and feel the gentle
breeze.

3. And when I think that God, his Son not
sparing,
sent him to die, I scarce can take it in
that on the cross, my burden gladly
bearing,
he bled and died to take away my sin.

4. When Christ shall come with shout of
acclamation,
and take me home, what joy shall fill my
heart;
then I shall bow in humble adoration,
and there proclaim: my God, how great
thou art.

279 Philip Lawson Johnston
© 1982 Kingsway's Thankyou Music

1. O Lord our God, how majestic is your
name;
the earth is filled with your glory.
O Lord our God, you are robed in
majesty;
you've set your glory above the heavens.

We will magnify, we will magnify
the Lord enthroned in Zion.
We will magnify, we will magnify
the Lord enthroned in Zion.

2. O Lord our God, you have established a
throne,
you reign in righteousness and splendour.
O Lord our God, the skies are ringing
with your praise;
soon those on earth will come to
worship.

Continued overleaf

3. O Lord our God, the world was made at
      your command,
   in you all things now hold together.
   Now to him who sits on the throne and
      to the Lamb
   be praise and glory and pow'r for ever.

280
Twila Paris
© 1988, 1990 Ariose Music/Mountain Spring Music

O Lord, you have been good,
you have been faithful to all generations;
O Lord, your steadfast love
and tender mercy have been our
   salvation. *(x2)*

For by your hand,
we have been fed
and by your Spirit,
we have been led.
O Lord, you have been good,
you have been faithful to all generations.
For by your hand,
we have been fed
and by your Spirit,
we have been led.
O Lord, Almighty God,
Father unchanging, upright and holy.

O Lord, you have been good,
you have been faithful,
you have been good,
you have been good,
you have been faithful,
you have been good.

281
Graham Kendrick
© 1986 Kingsway's Thankyou Music

O Lord, your tenderness,
melting all my bitterness,
O Lord, I receive your love.
O Lord, your loveliness,
changing all my ugliness,
O Lord, I receive your love.
O Lord, I receive your love,
O Lord, I receive your love.

282
Susie Hare
© 2001 Kevin Mayhew Ltd.

1. O Love that searches all my soul,
   create in me anew,
   a purified and contrite heart
   that searches after you.
   Jesus, there is no sweeter grace,
   nor such forgiveness known
   as in the humble hearts of those
   wherein your love is sown,
   wherein your love is sown.

2. O Love that washes all my sins,
   create in me anew,
   salvation's joy and peace restored
   as I abide in you.
   Jesus, there is no sweeter joy
   than that which grace revives,
   nor greater peace within my heart
   than heaven's love provides,
   than heaven's love provides.

3. O Love that lifts my voice to sing,
   create in me anew,
   a song that always fills my heart
   with thankfulness to you.
   Jesus, there is no sweeter song
   than that which breathes your name,
   and through eternity my praise
   will always be the same,
   will always be the same.

283
George Matheson (1842-1906)

1. O Love that wilt not let me go,
   I rest my weary soul in thee;
   I give thee back the life I owe,
   that in thine ocean depths its flow
   may richer, fuller be.

2. O Light that follow'st all my way,
   I yield my flick'ring torch to thee;
   my heart restores its borrowed ray,
   that in thy sunshine's blaze its day
   may brighter, fairer be.

3. O Joy that seekest me through pain,
   I cannot close my heart to thee;
   I trace the rainbow through the rain,
   and feel the promise is not vain
   that morn shall tearless be.

4. O Cross that liftest up my head,
   I dare not ask to fly from thee:
   I lay in dust life's glory dead,
   and from the ground there blossoms red
   life that shall endless be.

284 George Bennard (1873-1958)
© The Rodeheaver Co./ Word Music
Administered by CopyCare

1. On a hill far away
   stood an old rugged cross,
   the emblem of suff'ring and shame;
   and I loved that old cross
   where the dearest and best
   for a world of lost sinners was slain.

   So I'll cherish the old rugged cross,
   till my trophies at last I lay down;
   I will cling to the old rugged cross
   and exchange it some day for a crown.

2. O that old rugged cross,
   so despised by the world,
   has a wondrous attraction for me:
   for the dear Lamb of God
   left his glory above
   to bear it to dark Calvary.

3. In the old rugged cross,
   stained with blood so divine,
   a wondrous beauty I see.
   For 'twas on that old cross
   Jesus suffered and died
   to pardon and sanctify me.

4. To the old rugged cross
   I will ever be true,
   its shame and reproach gladly bear.
   Then he'll call me some day
   to my home far away;
   there his glory for ever I'll share.

285 Cecil Frances Alexander (1818-1895)

1. Once in royal David's city
   stood a lowly cattle-shed,
   where a mother laid her baby
   in a manger for his bed.
   Mary was that mother mild,
   Jesus Christ her little child.

2. He came down to earth from heaven
   who is God and Lord of all,
   and his shelter was a stable,
   and his cradle was a stall.
   With the poor, and mean, and lowly
   lived on earth our Saviour holy.

3. And through all his wondrous childhood
   he would honour and obey,
   love and watch the lowly maiden
   in whose gentle arms he lay.
   Christian children all must be
   mild, obedient, good as he.

4. For he is our childhood's pattern:
   day by day like us he grew;
   he was little, weak, and helpless;
   tears and smiles like us he knew;
   and he feeleth for our sadness,
   and he shareth in our gladness.

5. And our eyes at last shall see him,
   through his own redeeming love;
   for that child so dear and gentle
   is our Lord in heaven above;
   and he leads his children on
   to the place where he is gone.

286

Andy Park
© 1989 Mercy/Vineyard Publishing/CopyCare

One thing I ask, one thing I seek,
that I may dwell in your house, O Lord.
All of my days, all of my life,
that I may see you, Lord.

Hear me, O Lord, hear me when I cry;
Lord, do not hide your face from me.
You have been my strength,
you have been my shield,
and you will lift me up.

One thing I ask, one thing I desire,
is to see you, is to see you.

287

Gerrit Gustafson
© 1990 Integrity's Hosanna! Music/Kingsway's
Thankyou Music

Only by grace can we enter,
only by grace can we stand;
not by our human endeavour,
but by the blood of the Lamb.
Into your presence you call us,
you call us to come.
Into your presence you draw us,
and now by your grace we come,
now by your grace we come.

Lord, if you mark our transgressions,
who would stand?
Thanks to your grace we are cleansed
by the blood of the Lamb.
(Repeat)

288

Graham Kendrick
© 1998 Ascent Music

1. On the blood-stained ground, where the
      shadow falls,
   of a cross and a crown of thorns,
   I kneel down, I kneel down,
   I lift my eyes to a tear-stained face;
   who is this dying in my place?
   I kneel down, I kneel down.

I come just as I am,
this is my only plea,
one hope in which I trust,
this blood was shed for me.

2. As you wash the stains of my guilty heart,
   'til I'm clean in ev'ry part,
   I kneel down, I kneel down.
   Wash away my shame, my pain, my
      pride,
   ev'ry sin that I once denied,
   I kneel down, I kneel down.
   This is where I'll always come,
   this is where I'll always run,
   to worship you, Jesus.
   This is where I'll always come,
   this is where I'll always run,
   to worship you, Jesus.

289

Henry Williams Baker (1821-1877)
based on Psalms 148 and 150, alt.

1. O praise ye the Lord!
   praise him in the height;
   rejoice in his word, ye angels of light;
   ye heavens, adore him,
   by whom ye were made,
   and worship before him,
   in brightness arrayed.

2. O praise ye the Lord!
   praise him upon earth,
   in tuneful accord, all you of new birth;
   praise him who hath brought you
   his grace from above,
   praise him who hath taught you
   to sing of his love.

3. O praise ye the Lord!
   all things that give sound;
   each jubilant chord re-echo around;
   loud organs his glory
   forth tell in deep tone,
   and, sweet harp, the story
   of what he hath done.

4. O praise ye the Lord!
thanksgiving and song
to him be outpoured all ages along:
for love in creation,
for heaven restored,
for grace of salvation,
O praise ye the Lord!

290

Mal Pope
© 1989 Samsongs/Coronation Music
Publishing/Kingsway's Thankyou Music

1. O righteous God who searches minds
   and hearts,
   bring to an end the violence of my foes,
   and make the righteous more secure,
   O righteous God.

   Sing praise to the name of the Lord most high.
   Sing praise to the name of the Lord most high.
   Give thanks to the Lord who rescues me,
   O righteous God.

2. O Lord my God, I take refuge in you;
   save and deliver me from all my foes.
   My shield is God the Lord most high,
   O Lord my God.

291

Matt Redman
© 1999 Kingsway's Thankyou Music

   O sacred King, O holy King,
   how can I honour you rightly,
   honour that's fit for your name?
   O sacred friend, O holy friend,
   I don't take what you give lightly;
   friendship instead of disgrace.

   For it's the myst'ry of the universe;
   you're the God of holiness,
   and yet you welcome souls like me.
   And with the blessing of your Father's heart,
   you discipline the ones you love;
   there's kindness in your majesty.
   Jesus, those who recognise your pow'r
   know just how wonderful you are
   that you draw near.

292

Phil Rogers
© 1988 Kingsway's Thankyou Music

1. O, that you would bless me,
   and enlarge my borders,
   that your hand would be with me,
   O Lord, O Lord.
   O, that you would keep me,
   keep me from all evil,
   so that I may not be ashamed
   O Lord, O Lord.

   May your kingdom come,
   may your will be done
   on earth as it is in heaven;
   may your kingdom come,
   may your will be done, through me
   O Lord, O Lord.

2. O, that you would fill me,
   fill me with your Spirit,
   so that I may know your pow'r,
   O Lord, O Lord.
   O, that you would use me
   to fulfil your purposes,
   that through me your glory would shine,
   O Lord, O Lord.

293

Samuel Trevor Francis

1. O the deep, deep love of Jesus!
   Vast, unmeasured, boundless, free;
   rolling as a mighty ocean
   in its fullness over me.
   Underneath me, all around me,
   is the current of thy love;
   leading onward, leading homeward,
   to my glorious rest above.

2. O the deep, deep love of Jesus!
   Spread his praise from shore to shore,
   how he loveth, ever loveth,
   changeth never, nevermore;
   how he watches o'er his loved ones,
   died to call them all his own;
   how for them he intercedeth,
   watcheth o'er them from the throne.

Continued overleaf

3. O the deep, deep love of Jesus!
   Love of ev'ry love the best;
   'tis an ocean vast of blessing,
   'tis a haven sweet of rest.
   O the deep, deep love of Jesus!
   'Tis a heav'n of heav'ns to me;
   and it lifts me up to glory,
   for its lifts me up to thee.

294
Dave Bilbrough
© 1980 Kingsway's Thankyou Music

O the valleys shall ring with the sound of
   praise,
and the lion shall lie with the lamb.
Of his government there shall be no end,
and his glory shall fill the earth.
May your will be done,
may your kingdom come!
Let it rule, let it reign in our lives.
There's a shout in the camp as we answer
   the call:
Hail the King! Hail the Lord of lords!

295
Charles Wesley

1. O thou who camest from above
   the pure celestial fire to impart,
   kindle a flame of sacred love
   on the mean altar of my heart.

2. There let it for thy glory burn
   with inextinguishable blaze,
   and trembling to its source return
   in humble prayer and fervent praise.

3. Jesus, confirm my heart's desire
   to work and speak and think for thee;
   still let me guard the holy fire
   and still stir up thy gift in me.

4. Ready for all thy perfect will,
   my acts of faith and love repeat,
   till death thy endless mercies seal,
   and make the sacrifice complete.

296
Susie Hare
© 2001 Kevin Mayhew Ltd.

Our Father in heaven,
hallowed be your name,
your kingdom come,
your will be done
on earth as in heaven.
Give us today our daily bread.
Forgive us our sins
as we forgive those who sin against us.
Lead us not into temptation,
but deliver us from evil.
For the kingdom, the power and the
   glory are yours,
now and for ever, now and for ever,
now and for ever. Amen.

297
Brenton Brown
© 1998 Vineyard Songs (UK/Eire)

1. Over all the earth, you reign on high,
   ev'ry mountain stream, ev'ry sunset sky.
   But my one request, Lord, my only aim
   is that you'd reign in me again.

   Lord, reign in me, reign in your pow'r;
   over all my dreams, in my darkest hour.
   You are the Lord of all I am,
   so won't you reign in me again.

2. Over ev'ry thought, over ev'ry word,
   may my life reflect the beauty of my Lord;
   'cause you mean more to me than any
      earthly thing,
   so won't you reign in me again.

298
Martin Smith
© 1994 Curious? Music UK/Kingsway's Thankyou
Music

Over the mountains and the sea
your river runs with love for me,
and I will open up my heart
and let the Healer set me free.
I'm happy to be in the truth,
and I will daily lift my hands,
for I will always sing of
when your love came down.

I could sing of your love for ever,
I could sing of your love for ever,
I could sing of your love for ever,
I could sing of your love for ever.

O, I feel like dancing,
it's foolishness, I know;
but when the world has seen the light,
they will dance with joy
like we're dancing now.

299
Noel Richards
© 1994 Kingsway's Thankyou Music

1. Overwhelmed by love,
   deeper than oceans,
   high as the heavens.
   Ever-living God,
   your love has rescued me.

2. All my sin was laid
   on your dear Son,
   your precious One.
   All my debt he paid,
   great is your love for me.

   No one could ever earn your love,
   your grace and mercy is free.
   Lord, these words are true,
   so is my love for you.

300 Robert Grant

1. O worship the King
   all glorious above;
   O gratefully sing
   his pow'r and his love:
   our shield and defender,
   the Ancient of Days,
   pavilioned in splendour,
   and girded with praise.

2. O tell of his might,
   O sing of his grace,
   whose robe is the light,
   whose canopy space;
   his chariots of wrath
   the deep thunder-clouds form,
   and dark is his path
   on the wings of the storm.

3. This earth with its store
   of wonders untold,
   almighty, thy pow'r
   hath founded of old:
   hath stablished it fast
   by a changeless decree,
   and round it hath cast,
   like a mantle, the sea.

4. Thy bountiful care
   what tongue can recite?
   It breathes in the air,
   it shines in the light;
   it streams from the hills,
   it descends to the plain,
   and sweetly distils
   in the dew and the rain.

5. Frail children of dust,
   and feeble as frail,
   in thee do we trust,
   nor find thee to fail;
   thy mercies how tender,
   how firm to the end!
   Our maker, defender,
   redeemer, and friend.

6. O measureless might,
   ineffable love,
   while angels delight
   to hymn thee above,
   thy humbler creation,
   though feeble their lays,
   with true adoration
   shall sing to thy praise.

301 John Samuel Bewley Monsell

1. O worship the Lord
   in the beauty of holiness;
   bow down before him,
   his glory proclaim;
   with gold of obedience,
   and incense of lowliness,
   kneel and adore him:
   the Lord is his name.

2. Low at his feet lay
   thy burden of carefulness:
   high on his heart
   he will bear it for thee,
   comfort thy sorrows,
   and answer thy prayerfulness,
   guiding thy steps
   as may best for thee be.

3. Fear not to enter
   his courts in the slenderness
   of the poor wealth
   thou wouldst reckon as thine:
   truth in its beauty,
   and love in its tenderness,
   these are the off'rings
   to lay on his shrine.

4. These, though we bring them
   in trembling and fearfulness,
   he will accept
   for the name that is dear;
   mornings of joy give
   for evenings of tearfulness,
   trust for our trembling
   and hope for our fear.

5. O worship the Lord
   in the beauty of holiness;
   bow down before him,
   his glory proclaim;
   with gold of obedience,
   and incense of lowliness,
   kneel and adore him:
   the Lord is his name.

302 Frances Jane van Alstyne (1820-1915)

1. Pass me not, O gentle Saviour,
   hear my humble cry;
   while on others thou art calling,
   do not pass me by.

   Saviour! Saviour!
   Hear my humble cry,
   and while others thou art calling,
   do not pass me by.

2. Let me at a throne of mercy
   find a sweet relief;
   kneeling there in deep contrition,
   help my unbelief.

3. Trusting only in thy merit,
   would I seek thy face;
   heal my wounded, broken spirit,
   save me by thy grace.

4. Thou the spring of all my comfort,
   more than life to me,
   whom have I on earth beside thee?
   whom in heav'n but thee?

303 Fred Chedgey © Mrs. Jean Chedgey

Peace I leave with you, be not afraid.
My peace I give you, be not afraid.
Peace I leave with you, be not afraid.
My peace I give you, be not afraid.
Not as the world gives do I give to you;
not as the world gives do I give to you.
Peace I leave with you, be not afraid.
My peace I leave you, be not afraid.

304 Trevor Burch © Trevor Burch

1. People awaken, open your eyes,
   see how the angels ride through the skies;
   darkness has ended, a new day has dawned,
   promised Messiah is born, God's only
     Son.

Light of the world, light from above,
God's revelation and gift of his love;
renew your birthplace here in my heart,
ever reign in me, never depart.

2. Child of the Father, bringer of peace
   to ev'ry soul that longs for release,
   bring us the liberty won on the tree,
   taking our sin, making us whole, setting
   us free.

3. The zeal of the Father has done great
       things -
   Jesus is risen with healing wings!
   Daystar eternal, rule from your throne,
   loving your people and leading them on.

305

Andy Piercy and Dave Clifton
© 1993 IQ Music Ltd.

Praise God, from whom all blessings flow,
praise him, all creatures here below.
Praise him above, you heav'nly host,
praise Father, Son and Holy Ghost.
    (Repeat)

Give glory to the Father,
give glory to the Son,
give glory to the Spirit
while endless ages run.
'Worthy the Lamb,' all heaven cries,
'to be exalted thus.'
'Worthy the Lamb,' our hearts reply,
'for he was slain for us.'
Praise God, from whom all blessings
    flow.
Praise God, from whom all blessings
    flow.
Praise God, from whom all blessings
    flow.
Praise God, from whom all blessings
    flow.

306

Frances Jane van Alstyne
(Fanny J. Crosby) (1820-1915)

1. Praise him, praise him!
   Jesus, our blessèd Redeemer!
   Sing, O earth,
   his wonderful love proclaim!
   Hail him, hail him!
   highest archangels in glory;
   strength and honour
   give to his holy name!
   Like a shepherd,
   Jesus will guard his children,
   in his arms he carries
   them all day long.
   Praise him, praise him!
   tell of his excellent greatness;
   praise him, praise him
   ever in joyful song!

2. Praise him, praise him!
   Jesus, our blessèd Redeemer!
   For our sins
   he suffered, and bled, and died!
   He – our rock,
   our hope of eternal salvation,
   hail him, hail him!
   Jesus the crucified!
   Sound his praises
   – Jesus who bore our sorrows,
   love unbounded, wonderful,
   deep and strong.

3. Praise him, praise him!
   Jesus, our blessèd Redeemer!
   Heav'nly portals,
   loud with hosannas ring!
   Jesus, Saviour,
   reigneth for ever and ever:
   crown him, crown him!
   Prophet, and Priest, and King!
   Christ is coming,
   over the world victorious,
   pow'r and glory
   unto the Lord belong.

307

Henry Francis Lyte (1793-1847), based on Psalm 103

1. Praise, my soul, the King of heaven!
   To his feet thy tribute bring;
   ransomed, healed, restored, forgiven,
   who like me his praise should sing?
   Praise him! Praise him!
   Praise him! Praise him!
   Praise the everlasting King!

2. Praise him for his grace and favour
   to our fathers in distress;
   praise him still the same as ever,
   slow to chide and swift to bless.
   Praise him! Praise him!
   Praise him! Praise him!
   Glorious in his faithfulness!

3. Father-like, he tends and spares us;
   well our feeble frame he knows;
   in his hands he gently bears us,
   rescues us from all our foes.
   Praise him! Praise him!
   Praise him! Praise him!
   Widely as his mercy flows!

4. Angels, help us to adore him;
   ye behold him face to face;
   sun and moon, bow down before him,
   dwellers all in time and space.
   Praise him! Praise him!
   Praise him! Praise him!
   Praise with us the God of grace!

309

John Henry Newman (1801-1890)

1. Praise to the Holiest in the height,
   and in the depth be praise;
   in all his words most wonderful,
   most sure in all his ways.

2. O loving wisdom of our God!
   When all was sin and shame,
   a second Adam to the fight
   and to the rescue came.

3. O wisest love! that flesh and blood,
   which did in Adam fail,
   should strive afresh against the foe,
   should strive and should prevail;

4. And that a higher gift than grace
   should flesh and blood refine,
   God's presence and his very self,
   and essence all-divine.

5. And in the garden secretly,
   and on the cross on high,
   should teach his brethren, and inspire
   to suffer and to die.

6. Praise to the Holiest in the height,
   and in the depth be praise;
   in all his words most wonderful,
   most sure in all his ways.

308

Roy Hicks
© 1976 Latter Rain Music/ EMI Christian Music Publishing/CopyCare

Praise the name of Jesus,
praise the name of Jesus,
he's my rock, he's my fortress,
he's my deliverer, in him will I trust.
Praise the name of Jesus.

310

Joachim Neander (1650-1680)
trans. Catherine Winkworth (1827-1878)

1. Praise to the Lord,
   the Almighty, the King of creation!
   O my soul, praise him,
   for he is thy health and salvation.
   All ye who hear,
   now to his temple draw near;
   joining in glad adoration.

2. Praise to the Lord,
   who o'er all things so wondrously reigneth,
   shieldeth thee gently from harm,
   or when fainting sustaineth:
   hast thou not seen
   how thy heart's wishes have been
   granted in what he ordaineth?

3. Praise to the Lord,
   who doth prosper thy work and defend thee,
   surely his goodness and mercy
   shall daily attend thee:
   ponder anew
   what the Almighty can do,
   if to the end he befriend thee.

4. Praise to the Lord,
   O let all that is in us adore him!
   All that hath life and breath,
   come now with praises before him.
   Let the 'Amen'
   sound from his people again,
   gladly for ay we adore him.

3. Praise you, Lord,
   you have borne the depths of sorrow;
   praise you, Lord,
   for your anguish on the tree;
   the nails that tore your body
   and the pain that tore your soul -
   praise you, Lord,
   your tears, they fell for me.

4. Praise you, Lord,
   you have turned our thorns to roses;
   glory, Lord, as the bloom upon your brow;
   the path of pain is hallowed,
   for your love has made it sweet -
   praise you, Lord,
   and may I love you now.

311
Nettie Rose
© 1977 Kingsway's Thankyou Music

1. Praise you, Lord,
   for the wonder of your healing;
   praise you, Lord,
   for your love so freely giv'n;
   outpouring, anointing,
   flowing in to heal our wounds -
   praise you, Lord,
   for your love for me.

2. Praise you, Lord,
   for your gift of liberation;
   praise you, Lord,
   you have set the captives free;
   the chains that bind are broken
   by the sharpness of your sword -
   praise you, Lord,
   you gave your life for me.

312
Brian Doerksen
© 1990 Mercy/Vineyard Publishing/CopyCare

1. Purify my heart,
   let me be as gold and precious silver.
   Purify my heart,
   let me be as gold, pure gold.

   Refiner's fire,
   my heart's one desire
   is to be holy,
   set apart for you, Lord.
   I choose to be holy,
   set apart for you, my master,
   ready to do your will.

2. Purify my heart,
   cleanse me from within and make me
     holy.
   Purify my heart,
   cleanse me from my sin, deep within.

313

Chris Bowater
© 1985 Sovereign Lifestyle Music Ltd.

Reign in me, Sov'reign Lord,
reign in me.
Reign in me, Sov'reign Lord,
reign in me.

Captivate my heart,
let your kingdom come,
establish there your throne,
let your will be done.

314

Graham Kendrick
© 1983 Kingsway's Thankyou Music

Rejoice! Rejoice! Christ is in you,
the hope of glory in our hearts.
He lives! He lives! His breath is in you,
arise a mighty army, we arise.

1. Now is the time for us
   to march upon the land,
   into our hands
   he will give the ground we claim.
   He rides in majesty
   to lead us into victory,
   the world shall see that Christ is Lord!

2. God is at work in us
   his purpose to perform,
   building a kingdom
   of power not of words,
   where things impossible
   by faith shall be made possible;
   let's give the glory to him now.

3. Though we are weak, his grace
   is ev'rything we need;
   we're made of clay
   but this treasure is within.
   He turns our weaknesses
   into his opportunities,
   so that the glory goes to him.

315

Charles Wesley (1707-1788)

1. Rejoice, the Lord is King!
   Your Lord and King adore;
   mortals, give thanks and sing,
   and triumph evermore.

   Lift up your heart, lift up your voice;
   rejoice, again I say, rejoice.

2. Jesus the Saviour reigns,
   the God of truth and love;
   when he had purged our stains,
   he took his seat above.

3. His kingdom cannot fail;
   he rules o'er earth and heav'n;
   the keys of death and hell
   are to our Jesus giv'n.

4. He sits at God's right hand
   till all his foes submit,
   and bow to his command,
   and fall beneath his feet.

316

Graham Kendrick and Chris Rolinson
© 1981 Kingsway's Thankyou Music

1. Restore, O Lord,
   the honour of your name,
   in works of sov'reign power
   come shake the earth again,
   that all may see,
   and come with rev'rent fear
   to the living God,
   whose kingdom shall outlast the years.

2. Restore, O Lord,
   in all the earth your fame,
   and in our time revive
   the church that bears your name.
   And in your anger,
   Lord, remember mercy,
   O living God,
   whose mercy shall outlast the years.

3. Bend us, O Lord,
where we are hard and cold,
in your refiner's fire:
come purify the gold.
Though suff'ring comes
and evil crouches near,
still our living God
is reigning, he is reigning here.

4. *as verse 1.*

317 Augustus Montague Toplady (1740-1778) alt.

1. Rock of ages, cleft for me,
let me hide myself in thee;
let the water and the blood,
from thy riven side which flowed,
be of sin the double cure:
cleanse me from its guilt and pow'r.

2. Not the labours of my hands
can fulfil thy law's demands;
could my zeal no respite know,
could my tears for ever flow,
all for sin could not atone:
thou must save, and thou alone.

3. Nothing in my hands I bring,
simply to thy cross I cling;
naked, come to thee for dress;
helpless, look to thee for grace;
tainted, to the fountain fly;
wash me, Saviour, or I die.

4. While I draw this fleeting breath,
when mine eyelids close in death,
when I soar through tracts unknown,
see thee on thy judgement throne;
Rock of ages, cleft for me,
let me hide myself in thee.

318 Adrian Howard and Pat Turner
© 1985 Restoration Music/Sovereign Music UK

1. Salvation belongs to our God,
who sits on the throne,
and to the Lamb.
Praise and glory, wisdom and thanks,
honour and power and strength.

Be to our God for ever and ever,
be to our God for ever and ever,
be to our God for ever and ever. Amen.

2. And we, the redeemed, shall be strong
in purpose and unity,
declaring aloud,
praise and glory, wisdom and thanks,
honour and power and strength.

319 Stuart Townend
© 1994 Kingsway's Thankyou Music

1. Say the word, I will be healed;
you are the great Physician,
you meet every need.
Say the word, I will be free;
where chains have held me captive,
come, sing your songs to me,
say the word.

2. Say the word, I will be filled;
my hands reach out to heaven,
where striving is stilled.
Say the word, I will be changed;
where I am dry and thirsty,
send cool, refreshing rain,
say the word.
His tears have fallen like rain on my life,
each drop a fresh revelation.
I will return to the place of the cross,
where grace and mercy pour from
heaven's throne.

Continued overleaf

3. Say the word, I will be poor,
that I might know the riches
that you have in store.
Say the word, I will be weak;
your strength will be the power
that satisfies the meek,
say the word.
The Lord will see the travail of his soul,
and he and I will be satisfied.
Complete the work you have started in me:
O come, Lord Jesus, shake my life again.

320 Edward Caswall (1814-1878)

1. See, amid the winter's snow,
born for us on earth below,
see, the Lamb of God appears,
promised from eternal years.

   Hail, thou ever-blessèd morn!
   Hail, redemption's happy dawn!
   Sing through all Jerusalem:
   Christ is born in Bethlehem!

2. Lo, within a manger lies
he who built the starry skies,
he who, throned in height sublime,
sits amid the cherubim.

3. Say, ye holy shepherds, say,
what your joyful news today;
wherefore have ye left your sheep
on the lonely mountain steep?

4. 'As we watched at dead of night,
lo, we saw a wondrous light;
angels, singing peace on earth,
told us of the Saviour's birth.'

5. Sacred infant, all divine,
what a tender love was thine,
thus to come from highest bliss,
down to such a world as this!

6. Teach, O teach us, holy child,
by thy face so meek and mild,
teach us to resemble thee
in thy sweet humility.

321 Michael Perry (1942-1996) © 1965 Mrs B. Perry/Jubilate Hymns

1. See him lying on a bed of straw:
a draughty stable with an open door;
Mary cradling the babe she bore -
the Prince of Glory is his name.

   O now carry me to Bethlehem
   to see the Lord appear to men -
   just as poor as was the stable then,
   the Prince of Glory when he came.

2. Star of silver, sweep across the skies,
show where Jesus in the manger lies;
shepherds, swiftly from your stupor rise
to see the Saviour of the world!

3. Angels, sing again the song you sang,
bring God's glory to the heart of man;
sing that Bethl'em's little baby can
be salvation to the soul.

4. Mine are riches, from your poverty;
from your innocence, eternity;
mine, forgiveness by your death for me,
child of sorrow for my joy.

322 Trevor Burch © Trevor Burch

1. See his kingdom growing,
hear the people's song;
lightened faces glowing,
finding they belong.
Living in his Spirit,
filled with pow'r and grace,
working for his coming,
looking for his face.

You are head, Lord Jesus,
of your Church on earth,
bringing restoration,
bringing us new birth;
so Jesus bring your Church to glory,
pure before your throne,
keep us faithful till the day
 that brings your kingdom in.

2. Build your Church, Lord Jesus,
   make your people strong,
   living lives of vict'ry,
   knowing they belong.
   Bring about your kingdom,
   reign in hearts and homes;
   through your Church responding
   let your will be done.

3. Jesus, build your kingdom,
   build, O Lord, in me
   as my roots go deeper,
   grafted to the tree.
   Purify my hands, Lord,
   mould my heart and will.
   When you come in glory,
   may I be serving still.

323 Mark Altrogge
© 1997 PDI Praise. Administered by CopyCare

1. Should he who made the stars
   be hung upon a tree?
   And should the hands that healed
   be driven through for me?
   Should he who gave us bread
   be made to swallow gall?
   Should he who gave us breath and life
   be slaughtered for us all?

   We sing your mercies,
   we sing your endless praises,
   we sing your everlasting love.
   We sing your mercies,
   we sing your endless praises,
   Sov'reign One who died,
   Sov'reign One who died for us.

2. Should he who is the light
   be cast into the dark?
   And should the Lord of love
   be pierced through his own heart?
   Should he who called us friends
   be deserted by us all?
   Should he who lived a sinless life
   be punished for our fall?

324 Graham Kendrick
© 1988 Make Way Music

1. Show your pow'r, O Lord,
   demonstrate the justice of your kingdom.
   Prove your mighty word,
   vindicate your name
   before a watching world.
   Awesome are your deeds, O Lord;
   renew them for this hour.
   Show your pow'r, O Lord,
   among the people now.

2. Show your pow'r, O Lord,
   cause your church to rise and take action.
   Let all fear be gone,
   powers of the age to come
   are breaking through.
   We your people are ready to serve,
   to arise and to obey.
   Show your pow'r, O Lord,
   and set the people free.

(Last time)
   Show your pow'r, O Lord,
   and set the people –
   show your pow'r, O Lord,
   and set the people –
   show your pow'r, O Lord,
   and set the people free.

325
Joseph Mohr trans. John Freeman Young

1. Silent night, holy night.
   All is calm, all is bright,
   round yon virgin mother and child;
   holy infant, so tender and mild,
   sleep in heavenly peace,
   sleep in heavenly peace.

2. Silent night, holy night.
   Shepherds quake at the sight,
   glories stream from heaven afar,
   heav'nly hosts sing alleluia:
   Christ the Saviour is born,
   Christ the Saviour is born.

3. Silent night, holy night.
   Son of God, love's pure light,
   radiant beams from thy holy face,
   with the dawn of redeeming grace:
   Jesus, Lord, at thy birth,
   Jesus, Lord, at thy birth.

326
Stuart Garrard
© 1994 Kingsway's Thankyou Music

1. Sing to the Lord with all of your heart;
   sing of the glory that's due to his name.
   Sing to the Lord with all of your soul,
   join all of heaven and earth to proclaim:

   You are the Lord, the Saviour of all,
   God of creation, we praise you.
   We sing the songs that awaken the dawn,
   God of creation, we praise you.

2. Sing to the Lord with all of your mind,
   with understanding give thanks to the King.
   Sing to the Lord with all of your strength,
   living our lives as a praise offering.

327
Charles Wesley (1707-1788)
based on Ephesians 6:10-18

1. Soldiers of Christ, arise,
   and put your armour on,
   strong in the strength which God supplies
   through his eternal Son.

2. Strong in the Lord of hosts,
   and in his mighty pow'r;
   who in the strength of Jesus trusts
   is more than conqueror.

3. Stand then in his great might,
   with all his strength endued;
   and take, to arm you for the fight,
   the panoply of God.

4. To keep your armour bright,
   attend with constant care,
   still walking in your Captain's sight
   and watching unto prayer.

5. From strength to strength go on,
   wrestle and fight and pray;
   tread all the pow'rs of darkness down,
   and win the well-fought day.

6. That, having all things done,
   and all your conflicts past,
   ye may o'ercome, through Christ alone,
   and stand entire at last.

328
Daniel Iverson
© 1963 Birdwing Music/EMI Christian Music
Publishing/CopyCare

Spirit of the living God,
fall afresh on me.
Spirit of the living God,
fall afresh on me.
Melt me, mould me,
fill me, use me,
Spirit of the living God,
fall afresh on me.

329

Graham Kendrick
© 1989 Make Way Music

1. Such love, pure as the whitest snow;
   such love weeps for the shame I know;
   such love, paying the debt I owe;
   O Jesus, such love.

2. Such love, stilling my restlessness;
   such love, filling my emptiness;
   such love, showing me holiness;
   O Jesus, such love.

3. Such love springs from eternity;
   such love, streaming through history;
   such love, fountain of life to me;
   O Jesus, such love.

330

Frances Ridley Havergal (1836-1879)

Use these words when the tune Nottingham (Tune 1) is used

1. Take my life, and let it be
   consecrated, Lord, to thee;
   take my moments and my days,
   let them flow in ceaseless praise.

2. Take my hands, and let them move
   at the impulse of thy love;
   take my feet, and let them be
   swift and beautiful for thee.

3. Take my voice, and let me sing
   always, only, for my King;
   take my lips, and let them be
   filled with messages from thee.

4. Take my silver and my gold;
   not a mite would I withhold;
   take my intellect, and use
   ev'ry pow'r as thou shalt choose.

5. Take my will, and make it thine:
   it shall be no longer mine;
   take my heart: it is thine own;
   it shall be thy royal throne.

6. Take my love; my Lord, I pour
   at thy feet its treasure-store;
   take myself, and I will be
   ever, only, all for thee.

330

Frances Ridley Havergal (1836-1879)

Use these words when tune 2 is used.

1. Take my life, and let it be
   consecrated, Lord, to thee;
   take my hands, and let them move
   at the impulse of thy love,
   at the impulse of thy love.

2. Take my feet, and let them be
   swift and beautiful for thee.
   Take my voice, and let me sing
   always, only, for my King,
   always, only, for my King.

3. Take my lips, and let them be
   filled with messages from thee.
   Take my silver and my gold,
   not a mite would I withhold,
   not a mite would I withhold.

4. Take my love; my God I pour
   at thy feet its treasure-store.
   Take myself, and I will be
   ever, only, all for thee,
   ever, only, all for thee.

5. Take my life, and let it be
   consecrated, Lord, to thee.
   Take myself, and I will be
   ever, only, all for thee,
   ever, only, all for thee.

331

Graham Kendrick and Steve Thompson
© 1993 Make Way Music

Teach me to dance
to the beat of your heart,
teach me to move
in the pow'r of your Spirit,
teach me to walk
in the light of your presence,
teach me to dance
to the beat of your heart.
Teach me to love
with your heart of compassion,
teach me to trust
in the word of your promise,
teach me to hope
in the day of your coming,
teach me to dance
to the beat of your heart.

1. You wrote the rhythm of life,
   created heaven and earth,
   in you is joy without measure.
   So, like a child in your sight,
   I dance to see your delight,
   for I was made for your pleasure,
   pleasure.

2. Let all my movements express
   a heart that loves to say 'yes',
   a will that leaps to obey you.
   Let all my energy blaze
   to see the joy in your face;
   let my whole being praise you,
   praise you.

332

Timothy Dudley-Smith
© Timothy Dudley-Smith

1. Tell out, my soul,
   the greatness of the Lord!
   Unnumbered blessings,
   give my spirit voice;
   tender to me
   the promise of his word;
   in God my Saviour
   shall my heart rejoice.

2. Tell out, my soul,
   the greatness of his Name!
   Make known his might,
   the deeds his arm has done;
   his mercy sure,
   from age to age the same;
   his holy Name,
   the Lord, the Mighty One.

3. Tell out, my soul,
   the greatness of his might!
   Pow'rs and dominions
   lay their glory by.
   Proud hearts and stubborn wills
   are put to flight,
   the hungry fed,
   the humble lifted high.

4. Tell out, my soul,
   the glories of his word!
   Firm is his promise,
   and his mercy sure.
   Tell out, my soul,
   the greatness of the Lord
   to children's children
   and for evermore!

333

Martin Smith
1993 Curious? Music UK/Kingsway's Thankyou
Music

1. Thank you for saving me;
   what can I say?
   You are my ev'rything,
   I will sing your praise.
   You shed your blood for me;
   what can I say?
   You took my sin and shame,
   a sinner called by name.

   Great is the Lord.
   Great is the Lord.
   For we know your truth has set us free;
   you've set your hope in me.

2. Mercy and grace are mine,
   forgiv'n is my sin;
   Jesus, my only hope,
   the Saviour of the world.
   'Great is the Lord,' we cry;
   God, let your kingdom come.
   Your word has let me see,
   thank you for saving me.

334 Samuel John Stone

1. The church's one foundation
   is Jesus Christ, her Lord;
   she is his new creation,
   by water and the word;
   from heav'n he came and sought her
   to be his holy bride,
   with his own blood he bought her,
   and for her life he died.

2. Elect from ev'ry nation,
   yet one o'er all the earth,
   her charter of salvation,
   one Lord, one faith, one birth;
   one holy name she blesses,
   partakes one holy food,
   and to one hope she presses,
   with ev'ry grace endued.

3. 'Mid toil and tribulation,
   and tumult of her war,
   she waits the consummation
   of peace for evermore;
   till with the vision glorious
   her longing eyes are blest,
   and the great church victorious
   shall be the church at rest.

4. Yet she on earth hath union
   with God the Three in One,
   and mystic sweet communion
   with those whose rest is won:
   O happy ones and holy!
   Lord, give us grace that we
   like them, the meek and lowly,
   on high may dwell with thee.

335 Matt Redman and Martin Smith
© 1995 Kingsway's Thankyou Music

1. The cross has said it all,
   the cross has said it all.
   I can't deny what you have shown,
   the cross speaks of a God of love;
   there displayed for all to see,
   Jesus Christ, our only hope,
   a message of the Father's heart:
   'Come, my children, come home.'

   As high as the heav'ns are above the earth,
   so high is the measure of your great love;
   as far as the east is from the west,
   so far have you taken our sins from us.

2. The cross has said it all,
   the cross has said it all.
   I never recognised your touch
   until I met you at the cross;
   we are fallen, dust to dust,
   how could you do this for us?
   Song of God shed precious blood,
   who can comprehend this love?

   How high, how wide, how deep,
   how high, how wide, how deep,
   how high!

336 Martin Smith
© 1993 Kingsway's Thankyou Music

1. The crucible for silver,
   and the furnace for gold,
   but the Lord tests the heart of this child.
   Standing in all purity, God,
   our passion is for holiness:
   lead us to the secret place of praise.

   Jesus, Holy One, you are my heart's desire;
   King of kings, my ev'rything,
   you've set this heart on fire.

Continued overleaf

2. Father, take our off'ring,
   with our song we humbly praise you;
   you have brought your holy fire to our
      lips.
   Standing in your beauty, Lord,
   your gift to us is holiness:
   lead us to the place where we can sing:

337 John Ellerton (1826-1893)

1. The day thou gavest, Lord, is ended,
   the darkness falls at thy behest;
   to thee our morning hymns ascended,
   thy praise shall sanctify our rest.

2. We thank thee that thy Church
      unsleeping,
   while earth rolls onward into light,
   through all the world her watch is
      keeping,
   and rests not now by day or night.

3. As o'er each continent and island
   the dawn leads on another day,
   the voice of prayer is never silent,
   nor dies the strain of praise away.

4. The sun that bids us rest is waking
   our brethren 'neath the western sky,
   and hour by hour fresh lips are making
   thy wondrous doings heard on high.

5. So be it, Lord! Thy throne shall never,
   Like earth's proud empires, pass away;
   thy kingdom stands, and grows for ever,
   till all thy creatures own thy sway.

338 From William Sandys' 'Christmas Carols,
Ancient and Modern', alt.

1. The first Nowell the angel did say
   was to certain poor shepherds in fields as
      they lay:
   in fields where they lay keeping their sheep,
   on a cold winter's night that was so deep.

Nowell, Nowell, Nowell, Nowell,
born is the King of Israel!

2. They lookèd up and saw a star,
   shining in the east, beyond them far,
   and to the earth it gave great light,
   and so it continued both day and night.

3. And by the light of that same star,
   three wise men came from country far;
   to seek for a king was their intent,
   and to follow the star wherever it went.

4. This star drew nigh to the north-west,
   o'er Bethlehem it took its rest,
   and there it did both stop and stay
   right over the place where Jesus lay.

5. Then entered in those wise men three,
   full rev'rently upon their knee,
   and offered there in his presence,
   their gold and myrrh and frankincense.

6. Then let us all with one accord
   sing praises to our heav'nly Lord,
   who with the Father we adore
   and Spirit blest for evermore.

339 Thomas Olivers (1725-1799)
based on the Hebrew 'Yigdal', alt.

1. The God of Abraham praise,
   who reigns enthroned above,
   Ancient of everlasting Days,
   and God of love:
   Jehovah, great I Am,
   by earth and heav'n confessed;
   we bow and bless the sacred name,
   for ever blest.

2. The God of Abraham praise,
   at whose supreme command
   from earth we rise, and seek the joys
   at his right hand:
   we all on earth forsake,
   its wisdom, fame and pow'r;
   and him our only portion make,
   our shield and tow'r.

3. The God of Abraham praise,
whose all-sufficient grace
shall guide us all our happy days,
in all our ways:
he is our faithful friend;
he is our gracious God;
and he will save us to the end,
through Jesus' blood.

4. He by himself has sworn –
we on his oath depend –
we shall, on eagles' wings upborne,
to heav'n ascend:
we shall behold his face,
we shall his pow'r adore,
and sing the wonders of his grace
for evermore.

5. The whole triumphant host
give thanks to God on high:
'Hail, Father, Son and Holy Ghost!'
they ever cry:
Hail, Abraham's God and ours!
We join the heav'nly throng,
and celebrate with all our pow'rs
in endless song.

340 Judy Pruett
© 1990 Judy Pruett. Administered by Kingsway's
Thankyou Music

The grace of God upon my life
is not dependent upon me,
on what I have done or deserved,
but a gift of mercy from God
which has been given unto me
because of his love, his love for me.
It is unending, unfailing, unlimited,
    unmerited,
the grace of God given unto me.

341 Henry Williams Baker (1821-1877), based on Psalm 23

1. The King of love my shepherd is,
whose goodness faileth never;
I nothing lack if I am his
and he is mine for ever.

2. Where streams of living water flow
my ransomed soul he leadeth,
and where the verdant pastures grow
with food celestial feedeth.

3. Perverse and foolish oft I strayed,
but yet in love he sought me,
and on his shoulder gently laid,
and home, rejoicing, brought me.

4. In death's dark vale I fear no ill
with thee, dear Lord, beside me;
thy rod and staff my comfort still,
thy cross before to guide me.

5. Thou spread'st a table in my sight,
thy unction grace bestoweth:
and O what transport of delight
from thy pure chalice floweth!

6. And so through all the length of days
thy goodness faileth never;
good Shepherd, may I sing thy praise
within thy house for ever.

342 Graham Kendrick
© 1988 Make Way Music

1. *Men*   The Lord is a mighty King,
   Women   the Maker of ev'rything.
   Men   The Lord, he made the earth,
   Women   he spoke and it came at once
              to birth.
   Men   He said, 'Let us make
              mankind',
   Women   the crown of his design,
   Men   'in our own likeness',
   Women   his image in ev'ry human
              face.

And he made us for his delight,
gave us the gift of life,
created us family to be his glory,
to be his glory.

Continued overleaf

2.	*Men*	And yet we were deceived,
	Women	in pride the lie believed,
	Men	to sin and death's decay –
	Women	the whole creation fell that day.
	Men	Now all creation
	Women	yearns for liberation;
	Men	all things in Christ restored –
	Women	the purchase of his precious blood.

Shout:
For by him
all things were created.
Things in heaven
and on earth.
Visible and invisible.
Whether thrones
or powers
or rulers
or authorities;
all things were created by him,
and for him.

343 Graham Kendrick
© 1986 Kingsway's Thankyou Music

1. The Lord is marching out in splendour,
   in awesome majesty he rides,
   for truth, humility and justice,
   his mighty army fills the skies.

   O give thanks to the Lord
   for his love endures,
   O give thanks to the Lord
   for his love endures,
   O give thanks to the Lord
   for his love endures
   for ever, for ever.

2. His army marches out with dancing
   for he has filled our hearts with joy.
   Be glad the kingdom is advancing,
   the love of God, our battle cry!

344 Dan C. Stradwick
© 1980 Scripture in Song/Integrity Music/Kingsway's Thankyou Music

The Lord reigns, the Lord reigns,
the Lord reigns,
let the earth rejoice, let the earth rejoice,
let the earth rejoice,
let the people be glad that our God reigns.
(Repeat)

1. A fire goes before him
   and burns up all his enemies;
   the hills melt like wax at the presence of
     the Lord,
   at the presence of the Lord.

2. The heav'ns declare his righteousness,
   the peoples see his glory;
   for you, O Lord, are exalted over all the
     earth,
   over all the earth.

345 Stuart Townend, based on Psalm 23
© 1996 Kingsway's Thankyou Music

1. The Lord's my shepherd, I'll not want;
   he makes me lie in pastures green,
   he leads me by the still, still waters,
   his goodness restores my soul.

   And I will trust in you alone,
   and I will trust in you alone,
   for your endless mercy follows me,
   your goodness will lead me home.

2. He guides my ways in righteousness,
   and he anoints my head with oil;
   and my cup - it overflows with joy,
   I feast on his pure delights.

3. And though I walk the darkest path -
   I will not fear the evil one,
   for you are with me, and your rod and staff
   are the comfort I need to know.

346 The Scottish Psalter

1. The Lord's my shepherd, I'll not want.
   He makes me down to lie
   in pastures green. He leadeth me
   the quiet waters by.

2. My soul he doth restore again,
   and me to walk doth make
   within the paths of righteousness,
   e'en for his own name's sake.

3. Yea, though I walk in death's dark vale,
   yet will I fear none ill.
   For thou art with me, and thy rod
   and staff me comfort still.

4. My table thou hast furnishèd
   in presence of my foes:
   my head thou dost with oil anoint,
   and my cup overflows.

5. Goodness and mercy all my life
   shall surely follow me.
   And in God's house for evermore
   my dwelling-place shall be.

347 Susie Hare
© 2001 Kevin Mayhew Ltd.

1. The only power that cleanses me
   is in the blood of Jesus,
   and as I look to Calvary,
   his sacrifice I see.

   And anything that I might give
   would always be too small
   to ever pay the debt I owe
   to him who gave his life for me,
   to him who gave me all.

2. The only love that sets me free
   is in the heart of Jesus;
   a heart so full of tenderness
   and faithfulness to me.

3. I never cease to be amazed
   that he should love so dearly,
   a child of such unworthiness,
   a sinner such as me.

   So Jesus, take this thankful heart,
   although my gift is small.
   And I will live to worship you,
   because you gave your life for me,
   because you gave me all.

348 Graham Kendrick
© 1983 Kingsway's Thankyou Music

1. The price is paid,
   come, let us enter in
   to all that Jesus died
   to make our own.
   For every sin
   more than enough he gave,
   and bought our freedom
   from each guilty stain.

   The price is paid,
   alleluia,
   amazing grace,
   so strong and sure,
   and so with all my heart,
   my life in ev'ry part,
   I live to thank you
   for the price you paid.

2. The price is paid,
   see Satan flee away;
   for Jesus crucified
   destroys his pow'r.
   No more to pay,
   let accusation cease,
   in Christ there is
   no condemnation now.

Continued overleaf

3. The price is paid
   and by that scourging cruel
   he took our sicknesses
   as if his own.
   And by his wounds
   his body broken there,
   his healing touch may now
   by faith be known.

   The price is paid,
   alleluia,
   amazing grace,
   so strong and sure,
   and so with all my heart,
   my life in ev'ry part,
   I live to thank you
   for the price you paid.

4. The price is paid,
   'Worthy the Lamb!' we cry,
   eternity shall never
   cease his praise.
   The church of Christ
   shall rule upon the earth,
   in Jesus' name
   we have authority.

349 Cecil Frances Alexander (1818-1895)

1. There is a green hill far away,
   outside a city wall,
   where the dear Lord was crucified,
   who died to save us all.

2. We may not know, we cannot tell,
   what pains he had to bear,
   but we believe it was for us
   he hung and suffered there.

3. He died that we might be forgiv'n,
   he died to make us good;
   that we might go at last to heav'n,
   saved by his precious blood.

4. There was no other good enough
   to pay the price of sin;
   he only could unlock the gate
   of heav'n, and let us in.

5. O dearly, dearly has he loved,
   and we must love him too,
   and trust in his redeeming blood,
   and try his works to do.

350 F Whitfield

1. There is a name I love to hear,
   I love to speak its worth;
   it sounds like music in my ear,
   the sweetest name on earth.

   O how I love the Saviour's name,
   O how I love the Saviour's name,
   O how I love the Saviour's name,
   the sweetest name on earth.

2. It tells me of a Saviour's love,
   who died to set me free;
   it tells me of his precious blood,
   the sinner's perfect plea.

3. It tells of one whose loving heart
   can feel my deepest woe;
   who in my sorrow bears a part
   that none can bear below.

4. It bids my trembling heart rejoice,
   it dries each rising tear;
   it tells me in a still, small voice
   to trust and never fear.

351

Melody Green
© 1982 Birdwing Music/Ears to Hear Music/BMG
Songs Inc./EMI Christian Music Publishing/CopyCare

1. There is a Redeemer,
   Jesus, God's own Son,
   precious Lamb of God, Messiah,
   Holy One.

Thank you, O my Father,
for giving us your Son,
and leaving your Spirit
till the work on earth is done.

2. Jesus, my Redeemer,
   Name above all names,
   precious Lamb of God, Messiah,
   O` for sinners slain.

3. When I stand in glory,
   I will see his face.
   And there I'll serve my King for ever,
   in that Holy Place.

352
Ian White
© 1993 Little Misty Music. Administered by Kingsway's
Thankyou Music

1. There is holy ground to walk upon,
   there is peace that you can know;
   faith in God can fill your heart,
   and fear and doubt may go.
   There is holy ground to walk upon,
   leave behind your heavy shoes;
   come and stand in the shadow of his
     hands
   for he is calling you.
   Come and stand in the shadow of his
     hands,
   for he is calling you.

2. There is holy ground to walk upon,
   hear him beckon to the lame;
   for there his healing pow'r may flow,
   and limbs find strength again.
   There is holy ground to walk upon,
   there is holy work to do;
   trusting in the words of life,
   that Jesus births in you.
   Trusting in the words of life,
   that Jesus births in you.

3. There are holy dreams to dream upon,
   visions from the Lord on high;
   Jesus may be showing you,
   but will you turn your eyes?
   There is holy ground to walk upon,
   you can find the Jesus road;
   do not wait another day,
   but tell him you will go.
   Do not wait another day,
   but tell him you will go.

353
Robert Critchley
© 1993 Kingsway's Thankyou Music

There is one name under heaven
by which men can be saved,
Jesus alone.
Only one name under heaven,
Jesus, and Jesus alone.
One sacrifice, one holy Lamb
shed his own blood,
paid for my sin;
and this righteous One,
God's only Son,
I sing my praises to him,
I sing my praises to him.

354
Morris Chapman and Claire Cloninger
© 1990 Word Music Inc./Maranatha!Music/CopyCare

1. There is only one Lord that we cling to,
   there is only one truth that we claim;
   there is only one way that we walk in,
   there is only power in one name.

   And in the strong name of Jesus,
   by the blood of the Lamb,
   we are able to triumph,
   we are able to stand.
   In the power of his Spirit,
   by the strength of his hand,
   in the strong name of Jesus,
   by the precious blood of the Lamb.

Continued overleaf

2. Though apart from him we can do
nothing,
by his Spirit we can do all things;
covered by his blood we are made
righteous,
lifting up the name of Christ, our King!

355 Noel Richards
© 1989 Kingsway's Thankyou Music

1. There is pow'r in the name of Jesus;
we believe in his name.
We have called on the name of Jesus;
we are saved! We are saved!
At his name the demons flee.
At his name captives are freed,
for there is no other name that is higher
than Jesus!

2. There is pow'r in the name of Jesus,
like a sword in our hands.
We declare in the name of Jesus
we shall stand! We shall stand!
At his name God's enemies
shall be crushed beneath our feet,
for there is no other name that is higher
than Jesus!

356 Paul Oakley
© 1995 Kingsway's Thankyou Music

1. There's a place where the streets shine
with the glory of the Lamb.
There's a way, we can go there,
we can live there beyond time.

*Because of you, because of you,
because of your love,
because of your blood.*

2. No more pain, no more sadness,
no more suffering, no more tears.
No more sin, no more sickness,
no injustice, no more death.

Because of you . . .

*All our sins are washed away,
and we can live for ever,
now we have this hope,
because of you.
O, we'll see you face to face,
and we will dance together
in the city of our God,
because of you.*

3. There is joy everlasting,
there is gladness, there is peace.
There is wine everflowing,
there's a wedding, there's a feast.

357 Susie Hare
© 2001 Kevin Mayhew Ltd.

1. There's a time coming nearer that the
world waits to see,
there's a power that's moving to take
victory,
there's a new expectation of the
forthcoming days;
in the hearts of his people there's a new
song of praise.

*He is coming again the judge of the earth
for ever to reign.
He is coming again the judge of the earth
for ever to reign.
Prepare the way, prepare the way,
prepare the way of the Lord!
Prepare the way, prepare the way,
prepare the way of the Lord.*

2. When he rides on the heavens and he
shines like the sun,
when the trumpet has sounded and the
battle is won,
Satan's armies will perish and his
strongholds will fall
and the sound of rejoicing will drown
out his call.

3. Heaven's justice shall triumph over
   darkness and sin
   and a harvest of nations shall be gathered in;
   then the whole of creation will be held in
   his hand
   and a great celebration will sweep
   through this land.

358 Frederick Faber
© This version Jubilate Hymns

1. There's a wideness in God's mercy
   like the wideness of the sea;
   there's a kindness in his justice
   which is more than liberty.

2. There is no place where earth's sorrows
   are more keenly felt than heaven;
   there is no place where earth's failings
   have such gracious judgement giv'n.

3. There is plentiful redemption
   through the blood that Christ has shed;
   there is joy for all the members
   in the sorrows of the head.

4. For the love of God is broader
   than the measure of our mind,
   and the heart of the eternal
   is most wonderfully kind.

5. If our love were but more simple
   we should take him at his word,
   and our lives would be illumined
   by the glory of the Lord.

359 Robin Mark
© 1996 Daybreak Music Ltd.

1. These are the days of Elijah,
   declaring the word of the Lord;
   and these are the days of your servant, Moses,
   righteousness being restored.
   And though these are days of great trial,
   of famine and darkness and sword,
   still we are the voice in the desert crying,
   'Prepare ye the way of the Lord.'

Behold, he comes riding on the clouds,
shining like the sun at the trumpet call;
lift your voice, it's the year of jubilee,
out of Zion's hill salvation comes.

2. These are the days of Ezekiel,
   the dry bones becoming as flesh;
   and these are the days of your servant,
      David,
   rebuilding a temple of praise.
   These are the days of the harvest,
   the fields are as white in the world,
   and we are the lab'rers in your vineyard,
   declaring the word of the Lord.

360 Edith McNeil
© 1974 Celebration/Kingsway's Thankyou Music

The steadfast love of the Lord never ceases,
his mercies never come to an end.
They are new ev'ry morning,
new ev'ry morning;
great is thy faithfulness, O Lord,
great is thy faithfulness.

361 Dave Bilbrough
© 1996 Kingsway's Thankyou Music

1. The waves are breaking, the tide is
      turning,
   God's Spirit is coming to this earth;
   the harvest is waiting, and we have been
      called
   to go to the nations of this world.
   To the ends of the earth,
   to the ends of the earth,
   to the ends of the earth we will go;
   bearing the message that our God can be
      known,
   to the ends of the earth we will go.

Continued overleaf

2. The fire is falling, the wind is blowing,
the flame is spreading across our land;
revival is coming, let the world hear,
tell every woman, child and man.

To the ends of the earth,
to the ends of the earth,
to the ends of the earth we will go;
bearing the message that our God can be
* known,*
to the ends of the earth we will go.

3. The drums are beating, the trumpet is
sounding,
a warrior spirit he's put in our hearts;
in the name of the Father, Spirit and Son,
we'll take this word to ev'ryone.

362
Don Wallace
© 1998 PDI Worship. Administered by Copycare

The wonder of your mercy, Lord,
the beauty of your grace;
that you would even pardon me
and bring me to this place.
I stand before your holiness,
I can only stand amazed:
the sinless Saviour died to make
a covenant of grace.

1. I only want to serve you,
bring honour to your name,
and though I've often failed you,
your faithfulness remains.
I'll glory in my weakness,
that I might know your strength;
I will live my life at the cross of Christ,
and raise a banner to proclaim:

2. You welcome us before you,
into this holy place;
the brilliance of your glory
demands our endless praise.
The one, the only Saviour
has opened heaven's doors;
we can enter in, free from all our sin,
by your cleansing sacrifice.

363
Edmond Louis Budry trans. Richard Birch Hoyle
© Copyright control (revived 1996)

1. Thine be the glory,
risen, conqu'ring Son,
endless is the vict'ry
thou o'er death hast won;
angels in bright raiment
rolled the stone away,
kept the folded grave-clothes
where thy body lay.

Thine be the glory,
risen, conqu'ring Son,
endless is the vict'ry
thou o'er death hast won.

2. Lo! Jesus meets us,
risen from the tomb;
lovingly he greets us,
scatters fear and gloom.
Let the church with gladness
hymns of triumph sing,
for her Lord now liveth;
death hast lost its sting.

3. No more we doubt thee,
glorious Prince of Life;
life is naught without thee:
aid us in our strife.
Make us more than conqu'rors
through thy deathless love;
bring us safe through Jordan
to thy home above.

364
Graham Kendrick
© 1988 Make Way Music

1. This Child, secretly comes in the night,
O this Child, hiding a heavenly light,
O this Child, coming to us like a stranger,
this heavenly Child.

This Child, heaven come down now
to be with us here,
heavenly love and mercy appear,
softly in awe and wonder come near –
to this heavenly Child.

2. This Child, rising on us like the sun,
   O this Child, given to light everyone,
   O this Child, guiding our feet on the
      pathway
   to peace on earth.

3. This Child, raising the humble and poor,
   O this Child, making the proud ones to
      fall;
   O this Child, filling the hungry with
      good things,
   this heavenly Child.

365 Geoff Bullock

1. This grace is mine,
   this glory, earth-bound heaven sent
   this plan divine,
   this life, this light that breaks my night,
   the Spirit of God
   heaven falls like a dove to my heart.

2. This love is mine,
   so undeserved, this glorious name,
   this Son, this God,
   this life, this death, this vict'ry won,
   forgiveness has flowed and
   this grace that is mine finds my heart.

   The power and the glory of your name.
   The power and the glory of your name.
   The power and the glory of your name,
   the name of the Lord, the Son of God.

3. This life is mine,
   so perfect and so pure, this God in me,
   this glorious hope
   from earth to heaven, death to life,
   this future assured and secured
   by this love in my heart.

366 Marie Barnett

This is the air I breathe,
this is the air I breathe;
your holy presence living in me.
This is my daily bread,
this is my daily bread;
your very word spoken to me.

And I, I'm desp'rate for you.
And I, I'm lost without you.

367 Rick Shelton

1. This is the day that the Lord has made,
   I will rejoice and be glad in it;
   oh, this is the day that the Lord has made,
   I will rejoice and be glad in it.

   Rejoice in the Lord,
   rejoice in the Lord.

2. Celebrate the presence of the Lord,
   for he is worthy to be praised;
   celebrate the presence of the Lord,
   for he is worthy to be praised.

368 Matt Redman

This means I love you, singing this song,
Lord I don't have the words,
but I do have the will.
And this means I love you,
that I take up my cross,
I will sing as I walk out this love.

1. Jesus, this life is for you,
   ev'rything, Lord that I do;
   deeds that are pleasing and ways that are
      pure,
   Lord, may my life bear this fruit.

2. For these are the plans of my heart,
   yet often I'm missing the mark.
   See my desire to live in your truth;
   this surely means I love you.

369

Susie Hare
© 2001 Kevin Mayhew Ltd.

1. This side of heaven we know just in part,
   but then we will know with all of our
      heart;
   for what is unseen and what is unknown
   will one day to trusting hearts be shown.

   O what a day, O what a day, it will be!
   O what a sight, O what a sight we will see!
   O what a song, O what a song we will sing
   when we spend eternity worshipping Jesus
      the King!

2. This side of heaven, the things he has
      done
   are promises now of what is to come;
   he's leading us onward to all that is
      planned,
   when one day in glory we shall stand.

3. This side of heaven we're fixing our eyes
   on running the race and winning the prize;
   for we have been chosen and called by his
      grace,
   and one day we'll see him face to face.

   And nothing we've earned can take us
      there;
   the truth of our faith is sure,
   and only by mercy will we share
   his glorious home for evermore!

370

Emily Elizabeth Steele Elliott (1836-1897)
based on Luke 2:7
adapted by Michael Forster (b. 1946)
© This version copyright 1996 Kevin Mayhew Ltd.

1. Thou didst leave thy throne
   and thy kingly crown
   when thou camest to earth for me,
   but in Bethlehem's home
   was there found no room
   for thy holy nativity.

   O come to my heart, Lord Jesus,
   there is room in my heart for thee.

2. Heaven's arches rang
   when the angels sang
   and proclaimed thee of royal degree,
   but in lowliest birth
   didst thou come to earth
   and in deepest humility.

3. Though the fox found rest,
   and the bird its nest
   in the shade of the cedar tree,
   yet the world found no bed
   for the Saviour's head
   in the desert of Galilee.

4. Though thou cam'st, Lord,
   with the living word
   that should set all thy people free,
   yet with treachery,
   scorn and a crown of thorn
   did they bear thee to Calvary.

5. When the heav'ns shall ring
   and the angels sing
   at thy coming to victory,
   let thy voice call me home,
   saying, 'Heav'n has room,
   there is room at my side for thee.'

371

John Marriott (1780-1825) alt.

1. Thou, whose almighty word
   chaos and darkness heard,
   and took their flight;
   hear us, we humbly pray,
   and where the gospel-day
   sheds not its glorious ray,
   let there be light.

2. Thou, who didst come to bring
   on thy redeeming wing,
   healing and sight,
   health to the sick in mind,
   sight to the inly blind,
   O now to all mankind
   let there be light.

3. Spirit of truth and love,
   life-giving, holy Dove,
   speed forth thy flight;
   move on the water's face,
   bearing the lamp of grace,
   and in earth's darkest place
   let there be light.

4. Holy and blessèd Three,
   glorious Trinity,
   Wisdom, Love, Might;
   boundless as ocean's tide
   rolling in fullest pride,
   through the earth far and wide
   let there be light.

372 Psalm 34 in 'New Version' (Tate and Brady, 1696)

1. Through all the changing scenes of life,
   in trouble and in joy,
   the praises of my God shall still
   my heart and tongue employ.

2. O magnify the Lord with me,
   with me exalt his name;
   when in distress to him I called,
   he to my rescue came.

3. The hosts of God encamp around
   the dwellings of the just;
   deliv'rance he affords to all
   who on his succour trust.

4. O make but trial of his love:
   experience will decide
   how blest are they, and only they,
   who in his truth confide.

5. Fear him, ye saints, and you will then
   have nothing else to fear;
   make you his service your delight,
   your wants shall be his care.

6. To Father, Son and Holy Ghost,
   the God whom we adore,
   be glory as it was, is now,
   and shall be evermore.

373 Graham Kendrick
© 1998 Make Way Music

1. Through days of rage and wonder
   we pursue the end of time,
   to seize the day eternal,
   the reign of love divine.

2. Fixing our eyes on Jesus,
   we will press on day by day;
   this world's vain passing pleasures
   are not our destiny.
   Our ancient rites of passage
   still are the bread and wine:
   our hope a cross that towers
   over the wrecks of time.

3. Through days of rage and wonder,
   by the awesome pow'r of prayer
   God will shake ev'ry nation,
   secrets will be laid bare.
   And if his light increasing
   casts deeper shadows here,
   safe in his holy presence,
   love will cast out our fear.

4. Through days of rage and wonder
   you will give us grace to stand
   and seek a heav'nly city
   not built by human hands.
   Now is the only moment
   within our pow'r to change:
   to give back in obedience
   while life and breath remain.

374 James Wright
© 1996 Kingsway's Thankyou Music

1. Throughout the earth your glory will
      come,
   a day of pow'r, of salvation;
   to thirsty hearts your rivers will run,
   changing lives for the glory of God.
   From Satan's hold this land will be free,
   the deaf will hear, the blind will see;
   to walk in truth, in victory,
   to live for the glory of God.

Continued overleaf

Lord, come and reign
by the pow'r of your Spirit,
shower this land
with your rivers of life,
that Jesus the Son
would be glorified
within the heart of your Bride,
Lord, come and reign.

2. Upon the earth may your kingdom come,
within our lives may your will be done;
under the reign of Jesus the Son
we will live for the glory of God.
The gates of heaven are open wide,
to bless this land, to turn back the tide,
to welcome in your glorious Bride,
to live for the glory of God.

4. And we, shall we be faithless?
Shall hearts fail, hands hang down?
Shall we evade the conflict,
and cast away our crown?
Not so: in God's deep counsels
some better thing is stored:
we will maintain, unflinching,
one Church, one Faith, one Lord.

5. Thy mercy will not fail us,
nor leave thy work undone;
with thy right hand to help us,
the vict'ry shall be won;
and then by all creation,
thy name shall be adored.
And this shall be their anthem:
One Church, one Faith, one Lord.

375 Edward Hayes Plumptre (1821-1891) alt.

1. Thy hand, O God, has guided
thy flock, from age to age;
the wondrous tale is written,
full clear, on ev'ry page;
our forebears owned thy goodness,
and we their deeds record;
and both of this bear witness:
one Church, one Faith, one Lord.

2. Thy heralds brought glad tidings
to greatest, as to least;
they bade them rise, and hasten
to share the great King's feast;
and this was all their teaching,
in ev'ry deed and word,
to all alike proclaiming:
one Church, one Faith, one Lord.

3. Through many a day of darkness,
through many a scene of strife,
the faithful few fought bravely
to guard the nation's life.
Their gospel of redemption,
sin pardoned, hope restored,
was all in this enfolded:
one Church, one Faith, one Lord.

376 Charles Wesley (1707-1788)

1. 'Tis finished, the Messiah dies,
cut off for sins, but not his own.
Accomplished is the sacrifice,
the great redeeming work is done.
'Tis finished, all the debt is paid;
justice divine is satisfied,
the grand and full atonement made,
God for a guilty world hath died.

2. The veil is rent in Christ alone
the living way to heav'n is seen.
The middle wall is broken down
and ev'ryone may enter in.
The types and figures are fulfilled,
exacted in the legal pain;
the precious promises are sealed,
the spotless Lamb of God is slain.

3. The reign of sin and death is o'er
and all may live from sin set free.
Satan hath lost his mortal pow'r
'tis swallowed up in victory.
Saved from the legal curse I am,
my Saviour hangs on yonder tree;
see there the meek, expiring Lamb,
'tis finished! He expires for me.

4. Accepted in the well-beloved
   and clothed in righteousness divine,
   I see the bar to heav'n removed
   and all thy merits, Lord, are mine.
   Death, hell and sin are now subdued,
   all grace is now to sinners giv'n,
   and lo, I plead th' atoning blood
   and in thy right I claim thy heav'n.

377
Noel Richards
© 1991 Kingsway's Thankyou Music

1. To be in your presence,
   to sit at your feet,
   where your love surrounds me,
   and makes me complete.

   This is my desire,
   O Lord, this is my desire.
   This is my desire,
   O Lord, this is my desire.

2. To rest in your presence,
   not rushing away,
   to cherish each moment,
   here would I stay.

378
Frances Jane van Alstyne

1. To God be the glory!
   great things he hath done;
   so loved he the world
   that he gave us his Son;
   who yielded his life
   an atonement for sin,
   and opened the life-gate
   that all may go in.

   Praise the Lord, praise the Lord!
   let the earth hear his voice;
   praise the Lord, praise the Lord!
   let the people rejoice:
   O come to the Father,
   through Jesus the Son,
   and give him the glory;
   great things he hath done.

2. O perfect redemption,
   the purchase of blood!
   to ev'ry believer
   the promise of God;
   the vilest offender
   who truly believes
   that moment from Jesus
   a pardon receives.

3. Great things he hath taught us,
   great things he hath done,
   and great our rejoicing
   through Jesus the Son;
   but purer, and higher,
   and greater will be
   our wonder, our rapture,
   when Jesus we see.

379
Traditional South African
Translation © 1990 Wild Goose Publications

1. We are marching in the light of God,
   we are marching in the light of God.
   We are marching in the light of God,
   we are marching in the light of God.

   We are marching, marching,
   we are marching, oh, we are marching
   in the light of God.
   (Repeat)

2. We are living in the love of God . . .

3. We are moving in the pow'r of God . . .

380
Graham Kendrick
© 1986 Kingsway's Thankyou Music

1. We believe in God the Father,
   Maker of the universe,
   and in Christ his Son, our Saviour,
   come to us by virgin birth.
   We believe he died to save us,
   bore our sins, was crucified.
   Then from death he rose victorious,
   ascended to the Father's side.

Continued overleaf

Jesus, Lord of all, Lord of all,
Jesus, Lord of all, Lord of all,
Jesus, Lord of all, Lord of all,
Jesus, Lord of all, Lord of all.
Name above all names.
Name above all names.

2. We believe he sends his Spirit
on his church with gifts of pow'r.
God, his word of truth affirming,
sends us to the nations now.
He will come again in glory,
judge the living and the dead.
Ev'ry knee shall bow before him,
then must ev'ry tongue confess.

381 Brian Doerksen and Steve Mitchinson

We come to you with a heart of thanks,
for your love,
to be a living sacrifice, brought with love.
We come to you with a heart of thanks,
for your love;
an offering of all we are, brought with love.

All creation, looks to you;
all provision, comes from you.
In ev'ry sunrise, hope shines through.
For your mercy, we thank you.

We come to you with a song of praise,
for your love;
the music of our souls' delight, brought
with love.
We come to you with a song of praise,
for your love;
sounds of joy and gratefulness, brought
with love.

All creation looks to you.
All provision comes from you.
In ev'ry rhythm we thank you,
for your love.
All creation looks to you.
All provision comes from you.
In ev'ry season we thank you,
for your love.

382 Edward Joseph Burns (b. 1938)

1. We have a gospel to proclaim,
good news for all throughout the earth;
the gospel of a Saviour's name:
we sing his glory, tell his worth.

2. Tell of his birth at Bethlehem,
not in a royal house or hall,
but in a stable dark and dim,
the Word made flesh, a light for all.

3. Tell of his death at Calvary,
hated by those he came to save;
in lonely suff'ring on the cross:
for all he loved, his life he gave.

4. Tell of that glorious Easter morn,
empty the tomb, for he was free;
he broke the pow'r of death and hell
that we might share his victory.

5. Tell of his reign at God's right hand,
by all creation glorified.
He sends his Spirit on his Church
to live for him, the Lamb who died.

6. Now we rejoice to name him King:
Jesus is Lord of all the earth.
This gospel-message we proclaim:
we sing his glory, tell his worth.

383 Stuart Townend

1. We have sung our songs of vict'ry,
we have prayed to you for rain;
we have cried for your compassion
to renew the land again.
Now we're standing in your presence,
more hungry than before;
now we're on your steps of mercy,
and we're knocking at your door.

How long
before you drench the barren land?
How long
before we see your righteous hand?
How long
before your name is lifted high?
How long
before the weeping turns to songs of joy?

2. Lord, we know your heart is broken
   by the evil that you see,
   and you've stayed your hand of
       judgement
   for you plan to set men free.
   But the land is still in darkness,
   and we've fled from what is right;
   we have failed the silent children
   who will never see the light.

3. But I know a day is coming
   when the deaf will hear his voice,
   when the blind will see their Saviour,
   and the lame will leap for joy.
   When the widow finds a husband
   who will always love his bride,
   and the orphan finds a father
   who will never leave her side.

   How long
   before your glory lights the skies?
   How long
   before your radiance lifts our eyes?
   How long
   before your fragrance fills the air?
   How long
   before the earth resounds with songs of joy?

384

Isi de Gersigny
© 1981 Songs for the Nations. Administered by CopyCare

We lift up our eyes
above the troubles in our land,
and together we stand
to declare you as king.
In times like these we choose to praise you,
for it's you, it's you who really matter.

You are worthy of all praise,
and we will say that you are good,
and all the miracles you've done
have brought us joy,
for we are changed,
and all the hope we have
we place in you right now.
Father we declare that we love you.
We declare our everlasting love for you.
Father we declare that we love you.
We declare our everlasting love for you.

385

Graham Kendrick
© 1989 Make Way Music

1. We'll walk the land with hearts on fire;
   and ev'ry step will be a prayer.
   Hope is rising, new day dawning;
   sound of singing fills the air.

2. Two thousand years, and still the flame
   is burning bright across the land.
   Hearts are waiting, longing, aching,
   for awak'ning once again.

   Let the flame burn brighter
   in the heart of the darkness,
   turning night to glorious day.
   Let the song grow louder,
   as our love grows stronger;
   let it shine! Let it shine!

3. We'll walk for truth, speak out for love;
   in Jesus' name we shall be strong,
   to lift the fallen, to save the children,
   to fill the nation with your song.

386

Matthias Claudius (1740-1815)
trans. Jane Montgomery Campbell (1817-1878) alt.

1. We plough the fields and scatter
   the good seed on the land,
   but it is fed and watered
   by God's almighty hand:
   he sends the snow in winter,
   the warmth to swell the grain,
   the breezes and the sunshine,
   and soft, refreshing rain.

Continued overleaf

All good gifts around us
are sent from heav'n above;
then thank the Lord, O thank the Lord,
for all his love.

2. He only is the maker
   of all things near and far;
   he paints the wayside flower,
   he lights the evening star;
   he fills the earth with beauty,
   by him the birds are fed;
   much more to us, his children,
   he gives our daily bread.

3. We thank thee then, O Father,
   for all things bright and good:
   the seed-time and the harvest,
   our life, our health, our food.
   Accept the gifts we offer
   for all thy love imparts,
   and, what thou most desirest,
   our humble, thankful hearts.

3. We go in faith, our own great weakness
   feeling,
   and needing more each day thy grace to
   know:
   yet from our hearts a song of triumph
   pealing,
   'We rest on thee, and in thy name we go.'
   Yet from our hearts a song of triumph
   pealing,
   'We rest on thee, and in thy name we go.'

4. We rest on thee, our shield and our
   defender!
   Thine is the battle, thine shall be the praise;
   when passing through the gates of pearly
   splendour,
   victors, we rest with thee, through
   endless days.
   When passing through the gates of pearly
   splendour,
   victors, we rest with thee, through
   endless days.

387 Edith Gilling Cherry (1872-1897)

1. We rest on thee, our shield and our
   defender!
   We go not forth alone against the foe;
   strong in thy strength, safe in thy keeping
   tender,
   we rest on thee, and in thy name we go.
   Strong in thy strength, safe in thy
   keeping tender,
   we rest on thee, and in thy name we go.

2. Yes, in thy name, O captain of salvation!
   In thy dear name, all other names above;
   Jesus our righteousness, our sure
   foundation,
   our prince of glory and our king of love.
   Jesus our righteousness, our sure
   foundation,
   our prince of glory and our king of love.

388 Graham Kendrick
© 1988 Make Way Music

We shall stand
with our feet on the Rock.
Whatever they may say,
we'll lift your name up high.
And we shall walk
through the darkest night;
setting our faces like flint,
we'll walk into the light.

1. Lord, you have chosen me
   for fruitfulness,
   to be transformed
   into your likeness.
   I'm gonna fight on through
   till I see you face to face.

2. Lord, as your witnesses
you've appointed us.
And with your Holy Spirit
anointed us.
And so I'll fight on through
till I see you face to face.

389 Thomas Kelly (1769-1855)

1. We sing the praise of him who died,
of him who died upon the cross;
the sinner's hope all men deride,
for this we count the world but loss.

2. Inscribed upon the cross we see
in shining letters, 'God is love';
he bears our sins upon the tree,
he brings us mercy from above.

3. The cross! it takes our guilt away,
it holds the fainting spirit up;
it cheers with hope the gloomy day
and sweetens ev'ry bitter cup.

4. It makes the coward spirit brave,
and nerves the feeble arm for fight;
it takes the terror from the grave,
and gilds the bed of death with light.

5. The balm of life, the cure of woe,
the measure and the pledge of love;
the sinner's refuge here below,
the angels' theme in heav'n above.

390 Doug Horley
© 1993 Kingsway's Thankyou Music

We want to see Jesus lifted high,
a banner that flies across this land,
that all men might see the truth
and know he is the way to heaven.
(Repeat)

We want to see, we want to see,
we want to see Jesus lifted high.
We want to see, we want to see,
we want to see Jesus lifted high.

Step by step we're moving forward,
little by little taking ground,
ev'ry prayer a powerful weapon,
strongholds come tumbling down,
and down, and down, and down.

391 Reuben Morgan
© 1997 Reuben Morgan/Hillsongs Publishing/
Kingsway's Thankyou Music.

1. We will seek your face, almighty God,
turn and pray for you to heal our land.
Father, let revival start in us,
then ev'ry heart will know your kingdom
come.

Lifting up the name of the Lord,
in power and in unity.
We will see the nations turn.
Touching heaven, changing earth.
Lifting up the name of the Lord,
in power and in unity.
We will see the nations turn.
Touching heaven, changing earth.
Touching heaven, changing earth.

2. Never looking back we'll run the race,
giving you our lives we'll gain the prize.
We will take the harvest given us,
though we sow in tears, we'll reap in joy.

Send revival, send revival,
send revival to us.
(Repeat)

392 Joseph Medlicott Scriven (1819-1886)

1. What a friend we have in Jesus,
all our sins and griefs to bear!
What a privilege to carry
ev'rything to him in prayer!
O what peace we often forfeit,
O what needless pain we bear,
all because we do not carry
ev'rything to God in prayer!

Continued overleaf

2. Have we trials and temptations?
   Is there trouble anywhere?
   We should never be discouraged:
   take it to the Lord in prayer!
   Can we find a friend so faithful,
   who will all our sorrows share?
   Jesus knows our ev'ry weakness –
   take it to the Lord in prayer!

3. Are we weak and heavy-laden,
   cumbered with a load of care?
   Jesus only is our refuge,
   take it to the Lord in prayer!
   Do thy friends despise, forsake thee?
   Take it to the Lord in prayer!
   In his arms he'll take and shield thee,
   thou wilt find a solace there.

393

Bob Kauflin
© 1992 People of Destiny International/Word Music
Inc. Administerd by CopyCare

1. What a hope you have called us to,
   life for ever giving glory to you.
   Awaiting the day you make all things
      new;
   what a hope you have called us to.

2. Oh, the wealth you have given us,
   abundant grace and your righteousness,
   your wisdom, love and holiness.
   Oh, the wealth you have given us.

   More than we'd ask or imagine,
   far beyond our wildest dreams,
   all you've provided in Jesus Christ,
   with grateful hearts we receive,
   with grateful hearts we receive.

3. Oh, how great is your perfect might,
   deliv'ring us from the darkest night.
   Your holy pow'r to do what's right.
   Oh, how great is your perfect might.

394 Rufus H. McDaniel

1. What a wonderful change in my life has
      been wrought
   since Jesus came into my heart!
   I have light in my soul for which long I
      had sought,
   since Jesus came into my heart!

   Since Jesus came into my heart,
   since Jesus came into my heart,
   floods of joy o'er my soul
   like the sea billows roll,
   since Jesus came into my heart!

2. I have ceased from my wand'ring and
      going astray
   since Jesus came into my heart!
   And my sins which were many are all
      washed away
   since Jesus came into my heart!

3. I'm possessed of a hope that is steadfast
      and sure,
   since Jesus came into my heart!
   And no dark clouds of doubt now my
      pathway obscure,
   since Jesus came into my heart!

4. There's a light in the valley of death now
      for me,
   since Jesus came into my heart!
   And the gates of the city beyond I can
      see,
   since Jesus came into my heart!

5. I shall go there to dwell in that city, I
      know,
   since Jesus came into my heart!
   And I'm happy, so happy, as onward I go,
   since Jesus came into my heart!

395

Graham Kendrick
© 1994 Make Way Music

1. What kind of greatness can this be,
   that chose to be made small?
   Exchanging untold majesty
   for a world so pitiful.
   That God should come as one of us,
   I'll never understand.
   The more I hear the story told,
   the more amazed I am.

   O what else can I do
   but kneel and worship you,
   and come just as I am,
   my whole life an offering.

2. The One in whom we live and move
   in swaddling cloths lies bound.
   The voice that cried, 'Let there be light',
   asleep without a sound.
   The One who strode among the stars,
   and called each one by name,
   lies helpless in a mother's arms
   and must learn to walk again.

3. What greater love could he have shown
   to shamed humanity,
   yet human pride hates to believe
   in such deep humility.
   But nations now may see his grace
   and know that he is near,
   when his meek heart, his words, his works
   are incarnate in us.

396

Bryn and Sally Haworth
© 1983 Signalgrade/Kingsway's Thankyou Music

1. What kind of love is this
   that gave itself for me?
   I am the guilty one,
   yet I go free.
   What kind of love is this,
   a love I've never known?
   I didn't even know his name.
   What kind of love is this?

2. What kind of man is this
   that died in agony?
   He who had done no wrong
   was crucified for me.
   What kind of man is this
   who laid aside his throne,
   that I may know the love of God?
   What kind of man is this?

3. By grace I have been saved;
   it is the gift of God.
   He destined me to be his child,
   such is his love.
   No eye has ever seen,
   no ear has ever heard,
   nor has the heart of man conceived
   what kind of love is this.

397

Dave Bilbrough
© 1999 Kingsway's Thankyou Music

1. What love is this,
   that took my place?
   Instead of wrath,
   you poured your grace on me.
   What can I do
   but simply come
   and worship you?

   I surrender, I surrender, I surrender all to
   *   you.*

2. What love is this
   that comes to save?
   Upon the cross
   you bore my guilt and shame.
   To you alone
   I give my heart
   and worship you.

3. A greater love
   no man has seen;
   it breaks sin's pow'r
   and sets this pris'ner free.
   With all I have
   and all I am,
   I worship you.

398
Martin Leckebusch
© 2001 Kevin Mayhew Ltd.

1. What priceless treasures fill the hearts
   of all who are forgiven much,
   for grace is like the finest gold
   to those who feel God's loving touch:
   a debt removed, a heart made pure,
   a pardon sealed for evermore!

2. Forgiveness is the gift of God
   when harsher treatment would be right;
   the words which calm our gnawing guilt
   reveal the Father's chief delight -
   to tame and turn the rebel soul,
   to make the broken sinner whole.

3. If we deny our need of grace
   what foolish pride our words betray,
   since all the wrongs which we confess
   the blood of Christ will clean away:
   here justice and compassion meet -
   and here forgiveness is complete.

4. Released from sin's oppressive grasp,
   we make the way of grace our own
   as to each other we extend
   a pardon such as we have known:
   forgiven all, for ever free:
   what higher calling could there be?

399
Joseph Addison (1672-1719) alt.

1. When all thy mercies, O my God,
   my rising soul surveys,
   transported with the view, I'm lost
   in wonder, love and praise.

2. Unnumbered comforts to my soul
   thy tender care bestowed,
   before my infant heart conceived
   from whom those comforts flowed.

3. When in such slipp'ry paths I ran
   in childhood's careless days,
   thine arm unseen conveyed me safe,
   to walk in adult ways.

4. When worn with sickness oft hast thou
   with health renewed my face;
   and when in sins and sorrows sunk,
   revived my soul with grace.

5. Ten thousand thousand precious gifts
   my daily thanks employ,
   and not the least a cheerful heart
   which tastes those gifts with joy.

6. Through ev'ry period of my life
   thy goodness I'll pursue,
   and after death in distant worlds
   the glorious theme renew.

7. Through all eternity to thee
   a joyful song I'll raise;
   for O! eternity's too short
   to utter all thy praise.

400
Wayne and Cathy Perrin
© 1980 Integrity's Hosanna! Music

When I look into your holiness,
when I gaze into your loveliness,
when all things that surround become
   shadows in the light of you;
when I've found the joy of reaching your
   heart,
when my will becomes enthron'd in your
   love,

when all things that surround become
   shadows in the light of you:
I worship you, I worship you,
the reason I live is to worship you.
I worship you I worship you,
the reason I live is to worship you.

401
Isaac Watts

1. When I survey the wondrous cross
   on which the Prince of Glory died,
   my richest gain I count but loss,
   and pour contempt on all my pride.

2. Forbid it, Lord, that I should boast,
   save in the death of Christ, my God:
   all the vain things that charm me most,
   I sacrifice them to his blood.

3. See from his head, his hands, his feet,
   sorrow and love flow mingling down:
   did e'er such love and sorrow meet,
   or thorns compose so rich a crown?

4. Were the whole realm of nature mine,
   that were an offering far too small;
   love so amazing, so divine,
   demands my soul, my life, my all.

402 Matt Redman
© 1997 Kingsway's Thankyou Music

1. When the music fades,
   all is stripped away,
   and I simply come.
   Longing just to bring
   something that's of worth
   that will bless your heart.

   I'll bring you more than a song,
   for a song in itself
   is not what you have required.
   You search much deeper within,
   through the way things appear;
   you're looking into my heart.

   I'm coming back to the heart of worship,
   and it's all about you,
   all about you, Jesus.
   I'm sorry, Lord,
   for the thing I've made it,
   when it's all about you,
   all about you, Jesus.

2. King of endless worth,
   no one could express
   how much you deserve.
   Though I'm weak and poor,
   all I have is yours,
   ev'ry single breath.

   I'll bring you . . .

403 Robert Murray M'Cheyne (1813-1843) adapted by Pam Haworth
© 1997 Signalgrade/Kingsway's Thankyou Music

1. When this passing world is done,
   when has sunk the radiant sun,
   when I stand with Christ on high
   looking o'er life's history;
   when I hear the wicked call
   for the rocks and mountains to fall,
   then, Lord, shall I fully know,
   not till then, how much I owe.

2. When I stand before the throne
   dressed in beauty not my own,
   when I see you as you are,
   I'll love you with unsinning heart;
   when the praise of heav'n I hear
   loud as thunder to the ear,
   then, Lord, shall I fully know,
   not till then, how much I owe.

3. Chosen not for good in me,
   wakened up from wrath to flee,
   hidden in the Saviour's side,
   by the Spirit sanctified;
   here on earth, as through a glass,
   Jesus, let your glory pass;
   teach me, Lord, on earth to show,
   by my love, how much I owe.

404 John Henry Sammis
© 2001 Kevin Mayhew Ltd.

1. When we walk with the Lord in the light
      of his word,
   what a glory he sheds on our way!
   While we do his good will,
   he abides with us still,
   and with all who will trust and obey.

   Trust and obey, for there's no other way
   to be happy in Jesus, but to trust and obey.

Continued overleaf

2. Not a shadow can rise,
   not a cloud in the skies,
   but his smile quickly drives it away;
   not a doubt nor a fear,
   not a sigh nor a tear,
   can abide while we trust and obey.

   Trust and obey, for there's no other way
   to be happy in Jesus, but to trust and obey.

3. Not a burden we bear,
   not a sorrow we share,
   but our toil he doth richly repay:
   not a grief nor a loss,
   not a frown nor a cross,
   but is blest if we trust and obey.

4. But we never can prove
   the delights of his love
   until all on the altar we lay;
   for the favour he shows,
   and the joy he bestows,
   are for them who will trust and obey.

5. Then in fellowship sweet
   we will sit at his feet,
   or we'll walk by his side in the way;
   what he says we will do,
   where he sends we will go -
   never fear, only trust and obey.

405 Dave Bilbrough
© 1989 Kingsway's Thankyou Music

1. Who can ever say they understand
   all the wonders of his master plan?
   Christ came down and gave himself to
      man
   for evermore.

2. He was Lord before all time began,
   yet made himself the sacrificial lamb,
   perfect love now reconciled to man
   for evermore.

For evermore we'll sing the story of love
   come down,
For evermore the King of glory we will
   crown.

3. He is coming back to earth again,
   ev'ry knee shall bow before his name,
   'Christ is Lord', let thankful hearts
      proclaim
   for evermore.

4. (As verse 1)

406 Graham Kendrick
© 1988 Make Way Music

1. Who can sound the depths of sorrow
   in the Father heart of God,
   for the children we've rejected,
   for the lives so deeply scarred?
   And each light that we've extinguished
   has brought darkness to our land:
   upon our nation, upon our nation
   have mercy, Lord.

2. We have scorned the truth you gave us,
   we have bowed to other lords.
   We have sacrificed the children
   on the altar of our gods.
   O let truth again shine on us,
   let your holy fear descend:
   upon our nation, upon our nation
   have mercy, Lord.

(Men)
3. Who can stand before your anger?
   Who can face your piercing eyes?
   For you love the weak and helpless,
   and you hear the victims' cries.

(All)
   Yes, you are a God of justice,
   and your judgement surely comes:
   upon our nation, upon our nation
   have mercy, Lord.

(Women)

4. Who will stand against the violence?
   Who will comfort those who mourn?
   In an age of cruel rejection,
   who will build for love a home?

(All)

   Come and shake us into action,
   come and melt our hearts of stone:
   upon your people, upon your people
   have mercy, Lord.

5. Who can sound the depths of mercy
   in the Father heart of God?
   For there is a Man of sorrows
   who for sinners shed his blood.
   He can heal the wounds of nations,
   he can wash the guilty clean:
   because of Jesus, because of Jesus
   have mercy, Lord.

407 Susie Hare
© 2001 Kevin Mayhew Ltd.

1. Who, for my sake,
   so overwhelmingly suffered at Calvary;
   who, for my sake?
   Jesus the Lamb,
   in all his purity,
   slain on a cross to be Saviour of man.

   O, what grace to me flows so freely
   down from his throne above;
   where I should have been, in my place was
      seen,
   heaven's amazing love.

2. Who, for my sake,
   covered with holiness, all of my
      sinfulness;
   who, for my sake?
   Jesus the King,
   God's perfect sacrifice, yielded for me,
   his life, gave ev'rything.

408 Frances Ridley Havergal (1836-1879)

1. Who is on the Lord's side?
   Who will serve the King?
   Who will be his helpers
   other lives to bring?
   Who will leave the world's side?
   Who will face the foe?
   Who is on the Lord's side?
   Who for him will go?
   By thy call of mercy,
   by thy grace divine,
   we are on the Lord's side,
   Saviour, we are thine.

2. Jesus, thou hast bought us
   not with gold or gem,
   but with thine own life-blood,
   for thy diadem.
   With thy blessing filling
   each who comes to thee,
   thou hast made us willing,
   thou has made us free.
   By thy grand redemption,
   by thy grace divine,
   we are on the Lord's side,
   Saviour, we are thine.

3. Fierce may be the conflict,
   strong may be the foe,
   but the King's own army
   none can overthrow:
   round his standard ranging,
   vict'ry is secure;
   for his truth unchanging
   makes the triumph sure.
   Joyfully enlisting,
   by thy grace divine,
   we are on the Lord's side,
   Saviour, we are thine.

Continued overleaf

4. Chosen to be soldiers
   in an alien land,
   chosen, called, and faithful,
   for our captain's band;
   in the service royal
   let us not grow cold,
   let us be right loyal,
   noble, true and bold.
   Master, thou wilt keep us
   by thy grace divine,
   we are on the Lord's side,
   Saviour, always thine.

409
Paul Oakley
© 1995 Kingsway's Thankyou Music

Who is there like you,
and who else would give their life for me,
even suffering in my place?
And who could repay you?
All of creation looks to you,
and you provide for all you have made.

So I'm lifting up my hands,
lifting up my voice,
lifting up your name,
and in your grace I rest,
for your love has come to me
and set me free.
And I'm trusting in your word,
trusting in your cross,
trusting in your blood
and all your faithfulness,
for your pow'r at work in me
is changing me.

410
Graham Kendrick
© 1997 Make Way Music

1. Who sees it all, before whose gaze
   is darkest night bright as the day;
   watching as in the secret place
   his likeness forms upon a face?

2. Who sees it all, the debt that's owed
   of lives unlived, of love unknown?
   Who weighs the loss of innocence,
   or feels the pain of our offence?

   God sees, God knows,
   God loves the broken heart;
   and holds, and binds,
   and heals the broken heart.

3. Who knows the fears that drive a choice,
   unburies pain and gives it voice?
   And who can wash a memory,
   or take the sting of death away?

4. Whose anger burns at what we've done,
   then bears our sin as if his own?
   Who will receive us as we are,
   whose arms are wide and waiting now?

5. Whose broken heart upon a cross
   won freedom, joy and peace for us?
   Whose blood redeems, who ever lives
   and all because of love forgives?

411
Chris A. Bowater
© 1984 Sovereign Lifestyle Music

With a clean heart I'll praise you,
with a pure heart I'll honour you,
with a right spirit within me
I will magnify your name.
I will magnify your name,
I will magnify your name,
with a heart that's full of love for you
I will magnify your name.

412
John Pantry
© 1990 Harper Collins Religious. Administered by
Copycare Ltd.

1. Wonderful grace, that gives what I don't
      deserve,
   pays me what Christ has earned,
   then lets me go free.
   Wonderful grace, that gives me the time
      to change,
   washes away the stains that once covered
      me.

And all that I have
I lay at the feet
of the wonderful Saviour
who loves me.

2. Wonderful grace, that held in the face of
     death,
   breathed in its latest breath
   forgiveness for me.
   Wonderful love, whose pow'r can break
     ev'ry chain,
   giving us life again, setting us free.

413 Richard Baxter (1615-1691)
and John Hampden Gurney (1802-1862)

1. Ye holy angels bright,
   who wait at God's right hand,
   or through the realms of light
   fly at your Lord's command,
   assist our song,
   for else the theme
   too high doth seem
   for mortal tongue.

2. Ye blessèd souls at rest,
   who ran this earthly race,
   and now, from sin released,
   behold the Saviour's face,
   God's praises sound,
   as in his sight
   with sweet delight
   ye do abound.

3. Ye saints, who toil below,
   adore your heav'nly King,
   and onward as ye go
   some joyful anthem sing;
   take what he gives
   and praise him still,
   through good or ill,
   who ever lives.

4. My soul, bear thou thy part,
   triumph in God above:
   and with a well-tuned heart
   sing thou the songs of love;
   let all thy days
   till life shall end,
   whate'er he send,
   be filled with praise.

414 Charles Wesley (1707-1788)

1. Ye servants of God,
   your Master proclaim,
   and publish abroad
   his wonderful name;
   the name all victorious
   of Jesus extol;
   his kingdom is glorious,
   and rules over all.

2. God ruleth on high,
   almighty to save;
   and still he is nigh,
   his presence we have;
   the great congregation
   his triumph shall sing,
   ascribing salvation
   to Jesus our King.

3. 'Salvation to God
   who sits on the throne',
   let all cry aloud,
   and honour the Son:
   the praises of Jesus
   the angels proclaim,
   fall down on their faces,
   and worship the Lamb.

4. Then let us adore,
   and give him his right -
   all glory and pow'r,
   all wisdom and might:
   all honour and blessing,
   with angels above;
   and thanks never-ceasing,
   and infinite love.

415

A Simpson
© Copyright control

Yesterday, today, for ever,
Jesus is the same;
all may change, but Jesus never,
glory to his name!

Glory to his name!
Glory to his name!
All may change, but Jesus never,
glory to his name!

416

Brian Duane & Kathryn Scott
© 1999 Vineyard Songs

You are a holy God,
an all consuming fire.
You're robed in majesty,
bright, shining as the sun.

Your ways are not our ways.
Your thoughts are high above.
You are the fountain, Lord,
of mercy, truth and love.

(and we cry) 'Holy, holy is the Lord God
    most high.'
(and we cry) 'Holy, holy is the Lord most
    high.'

417

John Sellers
© 1984 Integrity's Hosanna! Music

You are crowned with many crowns,
and rule all things in righteousness.
You are crowned with many crowns,
upholding all things by your word.
You rule in power and reign in glory!
You are Lord of heaven and earth!
You are Lord of all.
You are Lord of all.

418

Don Moen
© 1997 Integrity's Hosanna! Music

You are my love and my light,
you are my purpose for living;
you are my hope in the night,
my reason for singing.
You bring a joy to my life,
and you're making it better and better;
and I will give thanks for ever and ever.

1. Will we ever know
   what we have been given?
   He has chosen us
   and called us his own.
   Flowing from his throne,
   there is a river;
   bringing life and health
   wherever it goes.

2. We will bless your name
   for always and ever,
   and offer up the sacrifices of praise.
   Teach us, Lord, we pray,
   to live in your presence;
   make us more and more
   like you ev'ry day.

419

Mavis Ford
© 1978 Word's Spirit of Praise Music/CopyCare

You are the King of Glory,
you are the Prince of Peace,
you are the Lord of heav'n and earth,
you're the Son of righteousness.
Angels bow down before you,
worship and adore, for
you have the words of eternal life,
you are Jesus Christ the Lord.
Hosanna to the Son of David!
Hosanna to the King of kings!
Glory in the highest heaven,
for Jesus the Messiah reigns.

420

1. You are the perfect and righteous God
   whose presence bears no sin;
   you bid me come to your holy place:
   how can I enter in
   when your presence bears no sin?
   Through him who poured out his life for
      me,
   the atoning Lamb of God,
   through him and his work alone
   I boldly come.

   I come by the blood, I come by the cross,
   where your mercy flows from hands pierced
      for me.
   For I dare not stand on my righteousness,
   my ev'ry hope rests on what Christ has done,
   and I come by the blood.

2. You are the high and exalted King,
   the One the angels fear:
   so far above me in ev'ry way.
   Lord, how can I draw near
   to the One the angels fear?
   Through him who laid down his life for me
   and ascended to your side,
   through him, through Jesus alone, I
      boldly come.

In your name there is mercy for sin,
there is safety within,
in your holy name.
In your name, there is strength to remain,
to stand in spite of pain,
in your holy name.

You are the sovereign 'I Am',
your name is holy.
You are the pure, spotless lamb,
your name is holy.
Your name is holy.

422

1. You have become for us wisdom,
   you have become for us righteousness.
   You have become our salvation,
   you have become all our holiness.

   All that we need is found in you,
   oh, all that we need is in you.
   All that we need is found in you;
   you are our all in all,
   you have become our all in all.

2. You have become our provision,
   in union with you we have victory.
   In you we have died and have risen,
   you are our great hope of glory.

421

You are the sovereign 'I Am',
your name is holy.
You are the pure, spotless lamb,
your name is holy.

You are the almighty one,
your name is holy.
You are the Christ, God's own Son,
your name is holy.

423

You laid aside your majesty,
gave up ev'rything for me,
suffered at the hands of those you had
   created.
You took all my guilt and shame,
when you died and rose again;
now today you reign,
in heav'n and earth exalted.

Continued overleaf

I really want to worship you, my Lord,
you have won my heart and I am yours
for ever and ever;
I will love you.
You are the only one who died for me,
gave your life to set me free,
so I lift my voice to you in adoration.

424
Darlene Zschech and Russell Fragar
© Darlene Zschech and Russell Fragar/Hillsongs
Publishing/Kingsway's Thankyou Music

1. You make your face to shine on me,
   and that my soul knows very well.
   You lift me up, I'm cleansed and free,
   and that my soul knows very well.

   When mountains fall I'll stand
   by the power of your hand
   and in your heart of hearts I'll dwell,
   and that my soul knows very well.

2. Joy and strength each day I find,
   and that my soul knows very well.
   Forgiveness, hope, I know is mine,
   and that my soul knows very well.

425
Mark Veary and Paul Oakley
© 1986 Kingsway's Thankyou Music

You, O Lord, rich in mercy,
because of your great love.
You, O Lord, so lov'd us,
even when we were dead in our sins.
You made us alive together with Christ,
and raised us up together with him
and seated us with him in heav'nly places
and raised us up together with him
and seated us with him in heav'nly places
   in Christ.

426
Darlene Zschech
© 1996 Darlene Zschech/Hillsongs Australia.
Administered by Kingsway's Thankyou Music

Your eye is on the sparrow,
and your hand, it comforts me.
From the ends of the earth
to the depths of my heart,
let your mercy and strength be seen.
You call me to your purpose,
as angels understand.
For your glory may you draw all men,
as your love and grace demands.

And I will run to you,
to your words of truth;
not by might, not by power
but by the Spirit of God.
Yes, I will run the race,
till I see your face.
Oh, let me live in the glory of your grace.

427
Stuart Townend
© 1999 Kingsway's Thankyou Music

1. Your love, shining like the sun,
   pouring like the rain,
   raging like the storm,
   refreshing me again;
   oh, I receive your love.

2. Your grace frees me from the past,
   it purges ev'ry sin,
   it purifies my heart
   and heals me from within;
   oh, I receive your grace.

   Pour over me,
   pour over me,
   let your rain flood this thirsty soul.
   Pour over me,
   your waves of love,
   pour over me.

3. I come and lay my burden down
   gladly at your feet.
   I'm op'ning up my heart,
   come make this joy complete;
   oh, I receive your grace.

Indexes

The Bridge

Index of Authors and Sources of Text

Scriptural Index

ACTS

Key Word Index

The key word categories appear alphabetically and are cross-referenced to make it as easy as possible for worship leaders to find songs and hymns suitable for various themes and occasions.

UNITY

See **Church – Fellowship and Unity**

VICTORY

VISION

WORD OF GOD

WORSHIP

See **Adoration and Praise**

Index of First Lines

The Bridge

Acknowledgements

The publishers wish to express their gratitude to the following for permission to include copyright material in this publication. Details of copyright owners are given above each individual hymn.

Ascent Music, PO Box 263, Croydon, CR9 5AP, UK. International copyright secured. All rights reserved. The songs 'No scenes of stately majesty' and 'On the bloodstained ground' are taken from *The Millennium Chorus*.

Ateliers et Presses de Taizé, F-71250, Taizé Communauté, France.

The Estate of A. C. Barham Gould, 34 Pollards Drive, Horsham, W. Sussex, RH13 5HH.

Mr Trevor Burch, Hill Country, St Aubin's Close, Four Marks, Alton, Hants, GU34 5DS.

Rev E. Burns, Christ Church Vicarage, 19 Vicarage Close, Fulwood, Preston, PR2 4EG.

Mr Phil Burt, 5 Gardner Road, Warton, Carnforth, Lancashire, LA5 9NW.

Mrs J. Chedgey, 40 Neville Close, Basingstoke, Hampshire, RG21 3HQ.

Christian Life Publications, PO Box 157, Bowles Well Gardens, Folkestone, Kent, CT20 2YS.

CopyCare, PO Box 77, Hailsham, East Sussex, BN27 3EF (music@copycare.com).

Daybreak Music Ltd., 4 Regency Mews, Silverdale Road, Eastbourne, East Sussex, BN20 7AB. International copyright secured. All rights reserved.

Mr Stuart Dauermann, 925 Beverly Way, Altadena, CA 91001, USA.

The Rt. Rev'd Timothy Dudley-Smith, 9 Ashlands, Ford, Salisbury, Wilts, SP4 6DY.

Far Lane Music, PO Box 2164, Florence, AL 35630, USA.

Free For Good, Bredon Fields, Eckington Road, Bredon, Tewkesbury, Glos, GL20 7HE. All rights reserved.

IQ Music Ltd., Commercial House, 52 Perrymount Road, Haywards Heath, W. Sussex, RH16 3DT.

Jubilate Hymns, 4 Thorne Park Road, Chelston, Torquay, TQ2 6RX.

Kingsway's Thankyou Music, PO Box 75, Eastbourne, East Sussex, BN23 6NW.

Leosong Copyright Service, Independent House, 54 Larkshall Road, Chingford, London, E4 6PD.

Make Way Music, PO Box 263, Croydon, CR9 5AP. International copyright secured. All rights reserved.

Novello and Company Ltd., 8/9 Frith Street, London, W1V 5TZ.

OCP Publications, 5536 NE Hassalo, Portland, OR 97213, USA. All rights reserved.

Oxford University Press, Gt. Clarendon Street, Oxford, OX2 6DP.

Restoration Music Ltd., PO Box 356, Leighton Buzzard, Beds., LU7 8WP.

Sovereign Lifestyle Music Ltd., PO Box 356, Leighton Buzzard, Beds., LU7 8WP.

Sovereign Music UK, PO Box 356, Leighton Buzzard, Beds., LU7 8WP.

TKO Publishing Ltd., PO Box 130, Hove, East Sussex, BN3 6QU. International copyright secured. All rights reserved.

Josef Weinberger Ltd., 12-14 Mortimer Street, London, W1N 7RD.

Wild Goose Resource Group, Iona Community, Pearce Institute, 840 Govan Road, Glasgow, G51 3UU.